KV-608-492

Ethics and Law in Health Care and Research

Edited by Peter Byrne

Department of Theology and Religious Studies
King's College, London, UK

JOHN WILEY & SONS
Chichester · New York · Brisbane · Toronto · Singapore

Copyright © 1990 by John Wiley & Sons Ltd.

Baffins Lane, Chichester

West Sussex PO19 1UD, England

This volume is a continuation of the King's College Studies series of
volumes previously published by King Edward's Hospital Fund for London.

Other Wiley editorial offices

John Wiley & Sons, Inc., 605 Third Avenue,
New York, NY 11158-0013, USA

Jacaranda Wiley Ltd, G.P.O. Box 859, Brisbane,
Queensland 4001, Australia

John Wiley & Sons (Canada) Ltd, 22 Worcester Road,
Rexdale, Ontario M9W 1L1, Canada

John Wiley & Sons (SEA) Pte Ltd, 37 Jalan Pemimpin 05-14,
Block B, Union Industrial Building, Singapore 2057

Library of Congress Cataloging-in-Publication Data

Ethics and law in health care and research/edited by Peter Byrne.
    p.   cm. — (King's College studies series)
  Includes bibliographical references.
  Includes index.
  ISBN 0 471 92806 2
  1. Medical ethics.   2. Medical ethics — Research — Law and
legislation. I. Byrne, Peter, 1950–   . II. Series.
  [DNLM: 1. Ethics, Medical.   2. Legislation, Medical.   3. Research.
W 50 E841]
  R724.E8213 1990
  174'.2 — dc20
  DNLM/DLC
  for Library of Congress   90-13504
                                                              CIP

British Library Cataloguing in Publication Data
Ethics and law in health care and research.
  1. Medicine. Ethical aspects
  I. Byrne, Peter, *1950–*
  174.2
  ISBN 0 471 92806 2

Typeset by Acorn Bookwork, Salisbury
Printed in Great Britain by Biddles Ltd., Guildford.

Ethics and Law
in Health Care and Research

Contents

Contributors

Michael Baum is Professor of Surgery, The Royal Marsden Hospital and the Institute of Cancer Research.

Sophie Botros is a Lecturer in Medical Ethics, Centre of Medical Law and Ethics, King's College, London.

Peter Byrne is a Lecturer in the Philosophy of Religion, King's College London.

Stephen Cretney is Professor of Law, University of Bristol.

Ian Kennedy is Professor of Medical Law and Ethics and a Director of the Centre of Medical Law and Ethics, King's College London.

Peter McCullagh works in the Department of Immunology, John Curtin School of Medical Research, Australian National University.

Caroline Miles is Director of the Ian Ramsey Centre, University of Oxford.

Sarah Spencer, formerly a General Secretary of Liberty (National Council for Civil Liberties), is a Research Fellow at the Institute of Public Policy Research, London.

Julie Stone is a Barrister and a Research Fellow at the Centre of Medical Law and Ethics, King's College London.

Preface

This is the fifth volume of essays in medical ethics and law that the King's College Centre of Medical Law and Ethics has presented to the public. As with previous volumes, the contributions are drawn from public lectures given in the College and invited papers from scholars within and outside the Centre. The essays reflect issues topical at the time they were written (the academic year 1988–9) and attempt to raise questions of enduring interest. As before, we have endeavoured to present a volume which is related to earlier ones in the series by way of continuity and difference.

New to this series is discussion of the ethics and epistemology of clinical research and the validation of novel therapies. Michael Baum offers a brief but typically challenging and clear statement of the difficulties of distinguishing between quackery and sound therapy. His account points to the manner in which the criteria of proof demanded by sound scientific methodology place strains on the accepted ethics of the doctor-patient relationship. Validation of therapies through controlled trials stands midway between research on animal or volunteer subjects, on the one hand, and standard medical practice, on the other. It is neither pure research nor pure therapy. The question he raises is whether the requirements of consent and non-maleficence routinely addressed in research and practice can be applied so easily to this hybrid. The intricate nature of the problems surrounding the definition of true consent and non-maleficence in the case of randomised trials is explored in great detail by Sophie Botros. Her chapter both introduces the reader to the wealth of literature on the ethics of clinical trials and takes the debate further through its careful analysis of the epistemology of clinical decisions and the ethical problems it raises. Peter McCullagh's paper not only treats the highly topical issue of the ethics of the use of fetal material for transplant, but serves as a concrete example of the problem highlighted by Professor Baum: namely, how can we distinguish between validated and non-validated therapies? It is a telling illustration of the way in which therapies can acquire the reputation of being worthwhile, regardless of any extensive evidence for that conclusion.

A recurrent theme of these volumes has been the role played by law, and the courts in particular, in commenting on and shaping medical practice. The next three chapters cover many varied issues in family and medical law, but are linked by a common theme of the problems faced by the law and the courts in shaping and executing public policy in this area. Stephen Cretney describes difficulties that beset both criminal and civil law in providing a framework within which the social, medical and psychiatric problems raised by the sexual abuse of children can be tackled. Julie Stone's chapter on access to infertility treatment shows how the courts, even with the resources of human rights law to draw upon, have little to say about justice in the availability of infertility treatment. In the absence, therefore, of any clearly argued and articulated public policy on these matters, the question of who exactly deserves medical support in starting a family through assisted reproduction tends to be settled by administrative or *ad hoc* decisions. This is a theme that she and Ian Kennedy then generalise in their study of recent decisions in medical law, which aims to bring out the haphazard way in which the state (in the United Kingdom) shapes medical practice. Their plea for a national commission for medical ethics and law can usefully be compared with the description by Alexander Capron of the prototype United States commission in the third volume of this series, *Health, Rights and Resources* (King's Fund Press/OUP, 1988).

Four themes broached in earlier volumes and treated anew here are: society's response to AIDS, resource allocation, the ethics of killing in medicine, and a mother's responsibilities to and rights over her unborn child. On the first, Sarah Spencer offers a valuable, specialist discussion of the civil liberties dimension of AIDS treatment, prevention and research. Caroline Miles explores the ins and outs of the UK government's attempts to import market forces into the provisions of a state-funded health care system. On the third theme, the editor endeavours to tie together discussions in earlier volumes of topics such as the sanctity of life and euthanasia. His particular concern is to introduce readers to the growing philosophical debate on the value of traditional distinctions which have been used to distinguish medical decisions resulting in hastened death from deliberate killing. On the final theme, Ian Kennedy offers reflections from jurisprudence which develop themes raised by John Eekelaar in *Health Rights and Resources*. Kennedy's discussion also bears on matters touched on by Peter McCullagh, namely how to determine the licit uses to which the human fetus can be put.

Peter Byrne

The ethics of clinical research

Michael Baum

Clinical reseachers come in for much criticism for their alleged use of patients as 'human guinea-pigs'. In deciding when, and how, to seek validation of new or untried therapies they in fact face an impossible dilemma. If they rigorously attempt comparative tests of new and existing therapies on patient-subjects, they will be accused of using the sick as instruments to gain knowledge. If they apply an unvalidated therapy to patients in general without previous controlled trials, they will be accused of taking risks with people's health. The only consistent rule that appears to be followed in public comment is that non-scientists and practitioners of 'alternative' medicine can do as they please. No doubt we shall continue to be treated to horror stories about human experiment and human 'guinea-pigs' but it is time we got down to examine the real nature of clinical research and its relation to successful clinical practice.

It is assumed very naively by many commentators that we conduct experiments on rats, mice and guinea-pigs, and having found the cure for the disease in an experimental animal we then *treat* people who suffer from that disease with the same remedy. Now a moment's reflection will tell you that this is obviously nonsensical, because in fact most animal models are not good models for human diseases. Or as Sir Michael Woodruff once said (private communication), 'We have the cure for cancer in rats and the only problem that remains is to persuade the rats to come to the clinics!' But when it comes to treatment of human subjects we have an enormous leap to make. There has to be some form of clinical research: there has to be the first treatment, and the first person with the new treatment.

Conventionally, we divide up human experimentation in medicine into four stages. The first stage is pre-clinical; this is basic research, and there clearly the subjects are volunteers. We then have three phases of clinical research. The first of these, phase one, is where we take a promising new drug, work out its dosimetry, its pharmacokinetics, its safety and the logistics of its delivery. That again is often done with healthy volunteers. We then come on to phase two, where we take this new therapy that looks safe and promising, and we use it with a group of patients suffering from perhaps the advanced stages of the disease and look for evidence of efficacy. Does the treatment influence the disease in any way? At this point we are not trying to discover if it is better than anything else, but simply whether it has biological and clinical activity. Again, the patients treated are usually volunteer subjects who understand that the treatment is purely experimental. The confusion arises when we come to phase three trials. We have a promising new approach, it does seem to work, but must ask: is it better or worse than conventional older treatments? That is where we enter the arena of the ethical dilemma that I want to address in this paper.

This dilemma is conditioned by a fundamental fact about modern medicine that cannot be overstressed. Much, if not most, of contemporary clinical practice is essentially based on forms of guesswork. Many accepted routine forms of treatment have not been properly scientifically validated. I passionately believe that the time has arrived when the guessing has to stop.

Therapeutic decision-making in modern medicine is a complicated area and the decision is arrived at partly from the viewpoint of the doctor and partly from the viewpoint of the patient. Let us first look at the way the patient approaches this decision-making. He or she will have expectations and often these expectations are quite unrealistic. Secondly, he or she may express priorities; for example, the priority that length of life is worth more than quality of life or vice versa. The patient may have fears; these fears may be rational or irrational, and some of these fears may be so great that he/she will refuse the recommended treatment if it is, for example, surgery or radiotherapy. And then the patient may wish to express different degrees of autonomy and self-determination. Many patients will say, 'I leave it all to you doctor, you decide'; but increasingly these days many better-informed patients say, 'I want to be involved in this decision-making'.

The doctor approaches the decision-making process from a

different viewpoint. First of all, 'What is the quality of evidence I can adduce that my favoured treatment is better than any other treatment available?' Secondly, 'If I favour this treatment, what about resource availability?' For example, if fast neutron therapy with a cyclotron is not available in south-east London and yet we felt it indicated, we would have to send the patient to Clatterbridge. Next, the ethical mode of the individual. This does not apply so much in my field, but there are certainly many areas where some doctors may feel that it is not ethical to strive officiously to keep alive. And finally, the doctor is entitled to, and usually does, calculate the utilities for the individual patient. The doctor may decide, for example, that this patient's length of life is not as important as this patient's quality of life.

For the purpose of this discussion I want to concentrate on the first imperative behind the doctor's decision, i.e. quality of evidence. I believe that modern medicine is a scientific discipline; it has its 'artistic' components as described above, but if we are not a science then I shudder to think what we are, because otherwise people are putting their trust in us to make life and death decisions based on intuition rather than empirical data. If I can say in one sentence my own perception of science, it would be to quote from Brecht in his life of Galileo: 'the aim of science is not to open the door to infinite wisdom but to set a limit to infinite error'[1].

Most of the progress in recent years in the treatment of the chronic diseases has been really to limit our error and limit the harm we do whilst waiting for the small breakthroughs which will ultimately reduce the total sum of human suffering. It is possible to construct a hierarchy of quality of evidence. At the weakest level of this hierarchy are anecdotal case reports and you can climb higher and higher via case control studies and database analysis; with each step your evidence as a scientist improves and strengthens until ultimately you can perform meta-analysis of multiple, confirmed, randomised clinical trials which will give you the strongest evidence in favour of one treatment over another. Another way of looking at this hierarchy, as a philosopher, is to recognise that the weakest evidence is purely inductive and is the type of evidence that is paraded in favour of alternative or quack remedies, and at the other extremes we have the powerful hypothetico-deductive approach of true scientific empiricism. But the problem with the powerful extreme of this hierarchy is that, in order to exclude bias, the trials have to include randomised controls, because the clinical trial, by having an unbiased control group to compare with the new treatment, recognises the clinician's prejudices, the clinician's fallibility and the very unpredictability of nature.

Having established the necessity for good science, good evidence and good clinical trials, we then have to address the difficult issue of informing the patient that a trial is going on, and here we can appeal to all sorts of international statements and declarations. The Nuremburg Convention, the MRC Statement, the Royal College of Physicians update on the MRC Statement, the BMA position and, the most famous of all, the Declaration of Helsinki[2]. Reading page 3 of the Declaration of Helsinki it seems pretty self-evident that in any research on human beings each potential subject should be adequately informed of the aims, methods, anticipated benefits and potential hazards of their study. The doctor should then attain that subject's freely given informed consent. Now, at this point most medical ethicists would consider the matter closed; they never turn over the page. Well within the Declaration of Helsinki we have the exclusion clause on the next page: 'If the doctor considers it essential not to obtain informed consent the specific reasons for this proposal should be stated in the experimental protocol'. So, I want to review for you very briefly the arguments that can be marshalled against informed consent and those that can be marshalled for informed consent, without attempting to take a position myself.

Against fully informed consent

Firstly, it is genuinely very difficult for patients to comprehend their disease and to comprehend the need for randomisation. Many of my patients are very frightened, and when you are frightened you have difficulty in understanding what people are saying to you. Next, you will undermine the confidence of your patient; if you tell the patient, 'Look I recommend this but I am guessing', or 'I am really not certain which of these two treatments is best for you', then he/she is likely to say, 'If you do not know what is best I will go to someone who does'. Patients will always find someone who knows what is 'best'; that is the frightening thing. Even when the experts do not know, the inexperts are *sure*. Informing patients of your uncertainty will cause distress and anxiety, and we do not want to hurt our patients; doctors try to be beneficent, and causing anxiety and distress is making patients ill. Many people believe that the patients get over their illness with a lot of support from their own inner resources, and you may damage those natural resources for self-healing if you frighten and distress them. Finally, you interfere with the doctor–patient relationship, particularly if a fee changes hands. You do not go to a private physician, pay a fee and then be told 'Well I do not know what is the best treatment for you, I will toss a coin.'

In favour of fully informed consent

You can marshal a set of counter arguments in favour of informed consent. The importance of respect for the other's right to self-determination is a categorical imperative. Improving the patient's knowledge of understanding of the illness and treatment is a further argument. If you explain the details of the clinical trial to a patient, his/her eyes light up and he/she says 'Now I understand the disease and now I understand why you want to treat it this way or the other'. If you involve patients in the decision-making process, then as well as showing respect for their autonomy you will also im-prove their compliance with therapy. Finally, there is litigation. Protecting the doctors from litigation does not apply in the UK because there is no law on seeking informed consent for random-isation in clinical trials. But in the United States of America there are laws in many states and much of the informed consent proce-dure in America is to protect the doctor rather than to protect the patient.

All the above is very theoretical and somewhat artificial. I want briefly to try to put flesh on this skeleton by explaining a particular trial that caused us a lot of soul searching.

The breast conservation trial

One must never underestimate the terror women experience when confronted with the diagnosis of breast cancer. This is a double anguish, the fear of premature death and the fear of a mutilating operation. Now, until 10 years ago we truly did not know whether the disease could be adequately treated by breast conservation (that is lumpectomy and radiotherapy), or whether in preserving the breast we risked the woman's life. But although the experts did not know, there were many surgeons who thought they knew with absolute confidence. The curious thing is that the surgeons who had all the answers had different answers and 10 years ago you would have surgeons who confidently believed that mastectomy was the best treatment, whereas you had an equal number of surgeons who confidently believed that lumpectomy and radiotherapy was the best treatment, and their behaviour was judged completely ethical. And yet it was a 50–50 chance whether you turned left or right in Harley Street, or whether you went to King's College Hospital or 'St Elsewhere', whether you had a mastectomy or a lumpectomy, but no one questioned the ethical standing of those doctors. However, there was another group of surgeons, the one who in fact knew a lot about the disease but did not know the answers, and they believed the only way to resolve these questions was to formally compare treatment by one or the other modality, in order ultimately to resolve the dilemma that has plagued us for the past 20 or 30 years. Yet that group of surgeons were judged as unethical because they wished to make formal comparisons. So we saw a double standard: if you wanted to make non-scientific comparisons amongst the patients of a group of bigots who thought they knew all the answers, that was ethical, but if you wanted to make any formal comparisons among the patients of a group of surgeons who were intellectually honest, that was judged to be unethical. To guide us out of this morass we recruited a lay ethicist to our working party for the first time. After three years of debate we launched the Cancer Research Campaign trial comparing mastectomy with lumpectomy and radiotherapy, and the guidelines we issued to our participants in order to get round all these ethical dilemmas were as follows.

The first step was to determine the patient's priorities. Did she in fact have a priority? Would she say (and it would be entirely legitimate for her to say so) 'I would rather lose my life than lose my breast'. If she felt that strongly she had the right to withdraw from the trial and have breast conservation. (Incidentally about 30% of the patients opted for *mastectomy* in this way.) If there were no expressed priorities, did the patient want to be involved in the decision-making process? If no, we felt that she had already expressed an autonomy, the autonomy not to be involved in the decision-making process. At that stage we would randomise. If yes, we would then explain all about the trial emphasising the good news, that the mere fact we had this dilemma was because they had a very good prognosis. If at that stage they expressed a preference they were excluded from the trial, but if they did not they were then randomised to either mastectomy or lumpectomy. Sadly we had to abort the trial after three years because we could not recruit: we frightened off most of the surgeons and we frightened off most of the patients. Meanwhile, women were still being treated by mastectomy or lumpectomy all around the country according to the random whim of the general practitioner's referral, or the leftness and rightness of their bias on walking down Harley Street. So what are we left with? We are really left with a balance of ethical imperatives that we cannot get right. On the one hand, we have the general ethical mode of the doctors which is one of beneficence; not only do we want to offer the best treatment available but we want to spare our patients unsolicited and potentially hurtful information. We like to consider the utilities of the patient. We may see thousands of such patients and therefore we can make a much more accurate judgement of the utilitarian outcomes than the individual patients facing up to the disease as an experience of one. We also have an ethical obligation to make progress for future generations so that the ravages of cancer can be reduced in the years to come. On the other hand, there is the consideration of the patient's autonomy and the right to self-determination, and the widespread acceptance of the prime importance of autonomy is now leading to the collapse of many important clinical trials in the USA and in the UK.

I would like to close with one thought, from a politician rather than a doctor. Paddy Ashdown, leader of the Liberal Democrats, in his 1988 address to their annual general meeting stated 'The essence of moral maturity lies not in the simplistic insistence that one value should have priority over all others, but in recognition that, as moral beings, we have constantly to face dilemmas, which cannot be resolved by reference to some *a priori* formula[3].

This statement of political philosophy certainly reflects my own attitude to the apparently irreconcilable demands of medical ethics and clinical research.

Notes and references

1. Bertolt Brecht, *Life of Galileo*, trans. John Willet, London: (Eyre Methuen, 1980) p. 176.
2. Declaration of Helsinki: recommendation guiding physicians in biomedical research involving human subjects (World Medical Association, 1981) Ferney-Voltaire.
3. Speech to SLD conference (Autumn 1988).

Equipoise, consent and the ethics of randomised clinical trials

Sophie Botros

A doctor has a duty to give his patient what he believes to be the best treatment. An ethical prerequisite of recommending her to enter a randomised clinical trial (RCT), in which his patient will be randomly allotted to one of two or more treatments, is, as Michael Baum in his chapter stresses, that he is ignorant about their relative efficacy and, hence, justifiably indifferent as to which she receives. Writers[1] who deny that a doctor's duty to his individual patient can be overriden by the need to advance science and so benefit future patients[2], commonly attack RCTs by asserting that rarely, even at the outset of an RCT, can a doctor be indifferent to the treatments being tested. Consequently recommending[3] his patient to enter an RCT will almost invariably contravene his duty to give her the treatment he believes to be the best.

Summary of the argument

My argument will be that this wholesale scepticism about the possibility of a doctor's indifference (due to ignorance) as to which treatment his patient receives, obscures the important distinction between situations in which patients are and those in which they are not prepared to make trade-offs between the advantages and disadvantages of particular treatments. Consider, for instance, a patient with breast cancer who does not discount the importance of prolongation of life when disfigurement is at stake. Though prior case histories may suggest that lumpectomy is as efficacious, in terms of survival, as mastectomy, the dubious evidential value of these histories means that a doctor really cannot, prior to an RCT, exclude the possibility that mastectomy may finally be found to be the better treatment for her.

But, as I shall indicate, a doctor's very scepticism as to the validity of the prior 'evidence' now raises embarrassing questions, for *supporters* of RCTs, concerning the permissibility of depriving patients, who have been randomly allotted to lumpectomy, of a treatment, such as mastectomy, with its acknowledged track record concerning survival. The source of this dilemma, I shall suggest, is the traditional polarisation of cognitive states into either knowledge or mere belief or 'opinion' which underlies current notions of equipoise. I finally propose a new approach, utilising ideas from Bayesian statistics, that allows the postulation of a grading of evidence as to the comparative value, all things considered, of two treatments, which is neither too weak nor too strong to exclude using RCTs.

Should, however, the requirements for a permissible RCT be thus far met (perhaps by utilising the Bayesian method), it might still be objected that it is wrong for doctors to allow their patients to submit to medical procedures whose primary aim is to advance knowledge and help future patients rather than to benefit the individual. I ask therefore whether obtaining a patient's informed consent could, as some writers believe[4], absolve the doctor of this deliberate failure to put his patients' interests first, and suggest that an affirmative answer depends upon a still controversial interpretation of the doctor–patient relationship. I consider (in the postscript) whether it is morally acceptable to use the Zellen method of pre-randomisation to minimise the requirement of informed consent for RCTs.

The charge of incompatibility

'The charge of incompatibility', as I shall term it, is broader than just the claim that a doctor may *sometimes* have to choose, during an RCT, whether to sacrifice his patient's interests to those of scientific progress as, for example, when a developing trend in the evidence, though not decisive statistically, nevertheless suggests that the treatment allotted to a patient may be harmful[5]. This dilemma, it is held, already confronts doctors at the outset of an RCT, and hence even before any trend might be apparent, since a doctor can never be genuinely indifferent as to which of the treatments being tested should be given to his patient. Fried suggests why this should be so in his pertinent question: 'Is it ever likely to be the case that in a complex medical situation the balance of harms and benefits discounted by their appropriate probabilities really does appear on the then available evidence to be in equipoise?'[6]

Schafer, developing Fried's point, suggests that frequently two treatments will only appear equivalent if the factors taken into account in assessing their comparative worth are restricted to gross measures, such as mortality and morbidity. Once, however, 'all the patient's circumstances, including his attitudes and value system are brought into the equation . . . the risks and benefits of the treatment alternatives will lose their equilibrium'.[7]

To illustrate their 'charge of incompatibility', critics of RCTs typically cite the following example. Suppose a doctor wishes to compare, as treatments for stage 1 breast cancer, mastectomy with lumpectomy. The doctor suspects that these treatments are of equal efficacy in terms of recurrence and survival, yet only one of them involves the removal of the whole breast and thus what many women would regard as serious disfigurement. To a patient randomly assigned to mastectomy, whom he knows fears disfigurement, he can promise no advantage in terms of survival compared with the women who receive the less aggressive therapy, mere removal of the lump. If the doctor *could* promise her longer survival, he could hardly morally justify allowing *other* patients to receive mere lumpectomy. But if he can promise her no advantage, how can he defend subjecting *her* to mastectomy, rather than patients who may care less about disfigurement or even wish for the removal of their 'offending' breast? Either quality of life is not to be taken into account in determining the better treatment (which seems unacceptable) or, if it is, we are faced with a doctor's apparently flagrant disregard of his patient's interests. As this is part of a deliberate attempt to gain knowledge for the benefit of the larger population of breast cancer sufferers, he may, with some justice, be described (to borrow a phrase from Baum's paper[8] as using his patient merely as an instrument for research.

But *defenders of RCTs*[9] will argue that, though a doctor has a duty to give his patient that treatment he believes to be the better, there would be no point in instituting an RCT if he already knew which it was. If he does not know which treatment is the better, and is hence in a state of 'clinical equipoise', how, in this situation, could he be charged, when entering his patient into an RCT, with violating his duty to give her the better treatment? Schafer's and Fried's position depends upon treating what is undoubtedly true for a few as if it were true for all patients. Of course some patients value the (certain or possible) advantages that one treatment offers so highly that they are not prepared to risk being allotted the other treatment. Consider, for instance, a woman who is not prepared to undergo mastectomy even when she is told that there is an 80% chance of surviving more than five years, and chooses to have a lumpectomy although she knows that there is no assured survival rate. Assuming that a doctor should take into account his patient's preferences in deciding which is the better treatment for her, this woman's doctor can already tell, even before the comparative survival rates for mastectomy and lumpectomy are known, that lumpectomy is, all things considered, the better treatment for her. Consequently, it would be quite indefensible for him to recommend her entry into an RCT in which she runs the risk of being randomly allotted mastectomy. Again, a doctor could not justifiably recommend a woman who simply wants to be rid of her 'offending' breast to enter an RCT of mastectomy against lumpectomy. Since she is quite uninterested in the suggestion that perhaps lumpectomy may prove as effective for survival as mastectomy, her doctor can already confirm that mastectomy is the better treatment for her.

But patients may frequently be prepared to make trade-offs between the advantages and disadvantages of treatments. Their position will be this: 'I will not discount the importance of the high chance of surviving at least five years which mastectomy promises and which, if lumpectomy turns out to have an inferior survival rate, will mean a greater prolongation of my life. But neither will I discount the chance that lumpectomy will be found to have the same survival rate as mastectomy and so I could escape disfigurement.' A doctor will be unable, prior to the RCT, to tell which is the better treatment, all things considered, for these patients and it will hence be justifiable for him to recommend them to enter it.

Fried's and Schafer's charge would only be convincing for these patients if comparisons, made before an RCT, of the relative merits (adjusted by their appropriate probabilities) of, for example, mastectomy and lumpectomy, were based upon *unbiased* estimates of the survival rates of the two treatments. But they cannot be; 'clinical equipoise' is precisely a state of indifference as to which of two treatments should be chosen *taking into account* the serious bias of estimates based on uncontrolled case histories and self-selected samples. It is, moreover, the very rejection by doctors and researchers of prior case histories as possessing a value as 'scientific evidence', and their determination to treat even estimates of probabilities based upon these as mere 'guesswork', that leads to the advocacy of RCTs.

That randomised treatment cannot be tailored to the patient's needs, though true, now loses much of its force. For, so long as doctors and researchers cannot give unbiased estimates for the survival rates of mastectomy as against lumpectomy, there is simply no valid account of the margin between survival rates for the treatments against which to balance the certain disadvantage of disfigurement. Hence even a detailed inquiry (as advocated by Schafer) into the priorities a particular patient assigns to, for example, prolongation of life against disfigurement, cannot, except in the instances detailed, help her doctor determine the better treatment for her. Consequently, in recommending her to enter an RCT, he does not sacrifice her right[10] to that treatment. Provided only that she is prepared to make *some* trade-off between prolongation of life and disfigurement, his advice to her must be that, even taking into account the known disadvantages to her of disfigurement, mastectomy could still turn out to be, all things considered, the better treatment for her. The claim that there is frequently a best treatment for a patient, when taking into account quality of life, besides survival and recurrence (which the RCT may demonstrate to be equal), should not be confused with the claim that a doctor can already tell before an RCT which is that treatment.

But *critics of RCTs* can now take up a different method of attack. If doctors and researchers when conducting RCTs feel justified in allowing *some* of their patients to forgo the officially more reputable or 'standard' treatment, especially when survival is at stake, then they must surely already have, to use Bradford Hill's words 'some basis' (eg. the results of past case histories, etc.)[11] for believing that, for instance, mastectomy is no more efficacious in terms of survival than lumpectomy. More than this, they must judge that they can *safely* omit the standard treatment. Indeed Bradford Hill remarks upon 'the impossibility of withholding, even temporarily, any treatment for a disease in which life and death is seriously at stake'. A measure, then, of just how confident doctors and researchers are, on the basis of informal evidence, that two treatments, such as mastectomy and lumpectomy, are equivalent in terms of survival is their readiness to run an RCT.

But if a doctor confidently expects women to survive just as long after either treatment, Fried's charge arises once again. For the doctor is then confronted with an uncomfortable choice: either to disregard the importance of quality of life, since this would tip the balance in favour of lumpectomy as the better treatment for those women who fear disfigurement, or, admitting the importance of quality of life, to allow these patients to be possibly randomised to the worse treatment for them, viz. mastectomy. In these latter circumstances, as we have seen, it would hardly be ethical for a doctor to recommend that these women enter the trial, unless it were also argued that patients' interests can sometimes be overriden in the interests of science and humanity.

Clinical equipoise: old and new interpretations

The real dilemma facing doctors and researchers wanting to run an RCT is that the very reasons in its favour also militate against it. There is evidence, tentative and biased, of the equal performance of mastectomy and lumpectomy in terms of survival which prompts doctors to run an RCT. But to justify allowing some women, who fear disfigurement, to be randomly allotted to mastectomy, when the prior evidence suggests it carries no advantage as regards survival over lumpectomy, the *unreliability* of this evidence has to be stressed. But if the evidence *is* unreliable how can doctors justify depriving those women who are randomly allotted to lumpectomy, or mastectomy, given its established record?

No illumination is shed on this problem, but rather it is further compounded by those writers who state that for RCTs to be permissible the doctor must believe that 'there is nothing to choose between the treatments'[12]. For this rendering of the notion of clinical equipoise is so loose as, ludicrously, to make it consistent with doctors having *proof* of the equal performance in terms of survival rates of two treatments which either have no, or equivalently disadvantageous, side-effects. The only plausible remaining interpretation of the statement is as a disclaimer of any knowledge as to the comparative efficacy of the treatments to be tested, and this has the difficulties we have already catalogued.

Some writers[13], borrowing the language of contemporary statistical methods to capture the notion of clinical equipoise, assert that the experimenter must be able 'to state an honest null hypothesis'. But this is just as ambiguous as previous attempts to render the idea of 'clinical equipoise'. For sometimes stating an honest null hypothesis is taken to exclude any belief at all about the comparative efficacy of the treatments being tested[14]. At other times, the null hypothesis is taken as consisting in a judgement that certain gross measures of outcome are equal, for example (in the comparison of mastectomy and lumpectomy), that five years after the initiating of either treatment, the probability that the patient will be alive is the same[15].

Again, we are pushed in one of two directions. To accept the latter interpretation may seem to countenance, prior to the trial, a kind of confidence concerning the comparable performance of the two treatments that is ethically incompatible with running the trial. To reject it in favour of the former interpretation is, as we saw, with other renderings of the notion of clinical equipoise, to invite the charge that we have too categorically dismissed the value of informal evidence, amassed at the outset of the trial and part of its *raison d'être*. But can we not avoid this kind of polarisation by postulating a quality of evidence which is neither too weak nor too strong to exclude a trial?

But all the versions of the notion of clinical equipoise that we have so far considered either embody, or are formulated against the background of, the traditional philosophical division between knowledge and proof, on the one hand, and opinion and belief, on the other. This stark division naturally cannot encompass the idea of subtle shifts and gradations in the strength of our evidence, and in the corresponding degrees of our confidence, before and after a trial. A few writers unenthusiastically attempt, from within this traditional cognitive framework, to give some slight weight to informal evidence, but many more appear to write it off. Gilbert[16], for instance, maintains that knowledge as to the comparative efficacy of treatments can only be achieved via randomised clinical trials, whilst statements made on the strength of uncontrolled studies must be regarded as 'ill-founded' and 'irrational'. They are nothing more than 'guesses' and hence 'likely to be wrong'. Indeed he cites experiments with highly intelligent students to confirm this view. Baum[17] too condemns 'much, if not most, of contemporary clinical practice [as] essentially based on forms of guesswork' and contrasts these with the scientific validation that can only be given by randomised clinical trials. 'The guessing' he says categorically 'has to stop'. Arthur Schafer[18] insists that since any treatment preference based on incomplete scientific knowledge 'falls well short of knowledge' it must be labelled 'bias or hunch'. V. Herbert[19], who admits that uncontrolled studies 'point in a direction', denies them the status of 'evidence' since only randomised clinical trials can 'tend to prove' or 'actually prove'. Even an authority of the stature of Bradford Hill, after uneasily allowing 'some' weight to the evidence without which he admits it would be impermissible to withhold an erstwhile standard treatment, nevertheless argues that, prior to a trial, a doctor 'really has no knowledge at all as to whether one treatment will be better or worse, safer or more dangerous than the other'. Again he emphasises that the doctor's state is one of 'ignorance' in which he believes the choice of treatments is 'a matter of indifference'[20]. To support this extreme claim, however, Bradford Hill has finally to discount data which earlier he was prepared to describe as 'some' evidence, as no evidence at all.

None of these writers apparently realises that their categorical dismissal of the value of informal evidence raises insuperable problems for the formulation of a notion of clinical equipoise that could make trials, such as that comparing mastectomy and lumpectomy, morally permissible. For their remarks simply invite the sceptical question: how could a physician justify denying to any woman suffering breast cancer the erstwhile 'standard' treatment (mastectomy), on the basis of mere guesswork, hunch or bias and when he is willing to admit that his views are so far 'irrational' and 'unfounded'? They meet Fried's and Schafer's charge but only at an unacceptable cost.

I have already suggested that our only hope of resolving this problem lies in being able to postulate a quality of evidence, and a corresponding degree of confidence in the comparable efficacy of treatments, such as mastectomy and lumpectomy, which is neither too strong nor too weak to exclude a trial. The validity of this evidence would not be undermined by, but rather acknowledged in, the decision to run a trial, during which our prior degree of confidence would be readjusted and more tightly focussed in the light of the new results. It is ironical, however, that amongst statistical methods, the practice that writers have seized upon, and erected into an ethical requirement of RCTs, namely that of stating a null hypothesis, is particularly unsuited to this approach. In the first place, the null hypothesis functions as a sceptical disclaimer of any prior knowledge of whether or not the treatments are equally efficaceous[21]. The thought behind its postulation is 'For all I know, there's no difference between the treatments – so let's test that'. But it is just this readiness to dismiss all prior evidence, and start, so to speak, *de novo*, that we are trying to avoid. Secondly, the point of stating a null hypothesis to the effect that the survival rates of two treatments, say mastectomy and lumpectomy, are the same is to devise a decision procedure, viz. the randomised clinical trial, for accepting or rejecting it[22]. But because the null hypothesis, which requires the survival rates to be precisely equated, is once-and-for-all confirmed or disconfirmed, there is no scope for re-adjustments of prior degrees of confidence concerning the comparability of the treatments (even were these expressible within the method).

There is an alternative Bayesian approach[23] which, though advocated by many theoretical statisticians today, has not yet found favour with medical researchers. Bayesians would get doctors to express their prior belief in a range of survival rates, or hypotheses, in terms of their confidence in each of them. In other words, they would get them to attach a subjective probability to each hypothesis, based on their own experience and that of published reports. The aim of the RCT would then be to concentrate the prior degree of confidence over a narrower range of possible survival rates. The Bayesian approach, in contrast to the classical statement of a null hypothesis, followed by a decision procedure for its outright rejection or acceptance, allows us to express a degree of confidence in our beliefs which, rather than having to be entirely set aside at the outset of the trial, can serve as a basis, which the results of the RCT will improve. A continuity can thus be established between our prior and our subsequent confidence, only varying in its degree of strength. The prerequisite for running an RCT would now be not 'clinical equipoise', but rather that doctors and researchers possess a degree of confidence as to the equivalence of the respective survival rates for two treatments, e.g. mastectomy and lumpectomy, strong *enough* but not *too* strong to justify an RCT. It would be an interesting project[23] to work out in greater detail how quantified prior confidence in the efficacy in terms of survival of two treatments, such as mastectomy and lumpectomy, which would take into account the biased data, could be balanced against the certain side-effects.

The role of consent in RCTs

I want finally to set the 'charge of incompatibility' in a wider context and consider where its rejection leads. The approach outlined above allows us, as we have seen, to postulate a quality of evidence, as to the comparative efficacy of two treatments, which is neither too weak nor too strong to prohibit an RCT. This quality of evidence permits a *certain* degree of confidence in the merits of one treatment over the other, but it is insufficient to justify doctors in identifying the better treatment. For this increased degree of certainty they must await the outcome of the RCT. Thus, since prior to the RCT a doctor cannot identify the better treatment, he does not, by recommending his patient to enter an RCT, jeopardise his duty to her to give her this treatment. Hence the 'charge of incompatibility' fails. Of course, if trends arise during the RCT indicating that one of the treatments being tested is better than the other, there will be a corresponding shift in the degree of confidence of doctors and researchers in the comparative merits of the two treatments which will preclude the continuation of the RCT.

Consider now a doctor who assesses the comparative merits of two treatments and concludes that, given the present state of his knowledge, he cannot say which is better. If either treatment had a disadvantage which the other lacked, and which the doctor were to deem relevant to his decision as to which was the better treatment, then, by hypothesis, he would already have taken it into account in assessing the comparative worth of the two treatments. May we not conclude then that it is permissible for him to recommend his patient to enter an RCT comparing the treatments? But is it right for a doctor to allow his patient to submit to a medical procedure whose object is primarily to benefit others, even when her chance of getting the better treatment is not jeopardised?

The answer depends upon our precise understanding of the duty which a doctor owes to his patient. Suppose this is a duty simply to give his patient what he believes to be the better treatment or, at least, not to put her at risk of receiving what he believes to be the worse treatment. A doctor, as we have seen, may fulfil this duty whilst recommending his patient to enter an RCT, although its primary aim is to benefit future patients rather than her individually.

But it is dangerous (for reasons I discuss in the postscript) to circumscribe the doctor's duty toward his patient in this way. If, however, we add that a doctor is also forbidden from doing to his patient, or allowing her to undergo, anything which is not primarily aimed at benefiting her, there are just two possibilities: either RCTs, even when a doctor genuinely does not know which is the better treatment for his patient, are impermissible, or obtaining a patient's informed consent to participation *makes* them permissible.

To claim that informed consent can make an otherwise impermissible RCT permissible is to give consent a role which goes beyond that which it plays in therapy. The patient's informed consent to a treatment is required to ensure that her doctor has neither subjected her to this treatment against her will nor manipulated her choice of treatment by concealing from her information about alternative treatments. But with RCTs there is yet a further danger. A patient could enter an RCT without realising that she will be subjected to medical procedures which are primarily aimed at benefiting future patients rather than herself. Her doctor might thus take advantage of her good faith that he will always put her interests first. Hence her informed consent to participate in an RCT is imperative.

But can a person, merely by giving consent, make another person's failure to fulfil his duty toward her any less wrong? Kantians show how autonomous persons can do this by waiving or alienating their rights. In their view, we are all, and not just doctors, morally prohibited from using people as '*mere* means' to our ends. Nevertheless an *autonomous* agent can *waive his right* not to be used by others for their ends. He will typically do so when he approves and wants to further these ends himself. Consequently, by consenting to being used by them for ends with which he either partly or wholly identifies, he absolves them of committing a wrong against him. Kantians would describe him as being used as a means but not, even should he suffer harm as a consequence, as a '*mere* means', to their ends[24]. Consider, for instance, a patient who consents, despite serious disadvantage to herself, to participate in an RCT because she wishes to do whatever she can to advance knowledge and so benefit future patients. She chooses to waive her right that her doctor put her interests first and thus absolves him of the wrong of failing to comply with his duty toward her.

But, it might be objected, patients are in no position to *waive* their rights. Indeed, on the traditional paternalistic conception of the doctor–patient relationship, the doctor's duty toward his patient does not arise out of a right on the part of his patient at all. In this respect it might be likened to the duties we owe animals or children or other persons who, because they lack autonomy, are often thought not to possess rights. Of course, if possessing rights were merely a matter of being owed other people's help or protection even persons of deficient autonomy (as patients are here regarded) could possess rights. But these would not be the kind of rights that the possessor could waive by an exercise of his autonomy. Many writers,[25] however, argue that a person cannot properly be described as possessing rights if he is not considered responsible enough to be able to choose to waive them. Hence they stipulate that we should speak only of the *duties* which other people owe such a person. Now, just as it does not make sense to suppose that such a person (a child would be a typical example) could release us from these duties, so it would seem inconceivable that the patient, on the traditional conception of the doctor–patient relationship, could so release her doctor.

The claim that a patient may, by consenting to participate in an RCT, absolve her doctor for any wrong he thus commits against her awaits, for its confirmation, the development of a new model on which to base the doctor–patient relationship. The new model would extend what is sometimes called a 'choice conception of rights' to the doctor–patient relationship. The patient's autonomy would then be regarded as capable of overriding considerations of beneficence, and hence it would be acknowledged that the doctor–patient relationship is one between equals.

The Zellen method of pre-randomisation: a postscript

Many doctors[26] are acutely aware of the conflict between their duty toward their individual patients and that which they owe to the larger population of future sufferers. To minimise this conflict, doctors and researchers who want to test a 'standard' treatment against, say, a combination of the 'standard' treatment and a new one, may use Zellen's[27] single pre-randomised design (as opposed to a symmetrical or double pre-randomised design[28]. This involves randomising patients *before* rather than *after* consent. Consent is then sought from those patients randomised to the 'standard plus' treatment; if they should refuse consent, they are assigned to the 'standard' treatment. But doctors argue that it is unnecessary to seek the consent of patients who have been allotted the 'standard' treatment since they will receive the 'recognised best' (i.e. the 'standard') treatment anyway. Doctors fear that, were these patients to learn that there existed an alternative treatment, which promises all the benefits of the 'standard' treatment combined with possible new benefits, they might refuse to take part in the RCT and, demanding the 'standard plus' treatment, prejudice the success of the trial.

There are several difficulties with Zellen's method of pre-randomisation as an ethically acceptable way of minimising the need for consent. First, if, as we have assumed, a doctor should generally take into account his patient's preferences in deciding which is the better treatment for her, the 'standard' treatment will not necessarily be the better treatment. For, as in the case under discussion, a patient may prefer an alternative treatment to the 'standard' treatment.

There are, of course, rare instances where having her preferences met would not be in a patient's best interests. Suppose, for instance, that a patient objects to being temporarily hospitalised though this may not only save her life but return her to full health. Or suppose that the patient herself acknowledges that what she wants is not what is in her best interests. So, she might tell her doctor that she wants a less aggressive treatment because fear of the more aggressive procedure haunts her. She is, however, quite willing to admit that the latter could ultimately be of longer benefit and hence that it is in her best interests to submit to it. But the patient's preference for the 'standard plus' treatment can hardly, in the example we are discussing, be dismissed as wayward or irrational since her doctor is prepared to submit half of his patients to it.

Second, it would seem wrong for a doctor, even when he thinks he knows which is the best treatment for his patient, to suppress from her information about alternative treatments. Doctors defend their action by arguing that if they were to tell a seriously ill patient about an alternative treatment which, though less aggressive than the treatment which they recommend, was in their opinion ineffective, she might put her life at risk by choosing it. They ask where they are to draw the line if they are obliged to inform patients even of such treatments? Should they, for instance, also tell their patients about quack 'cures' and 'natural' remedies, such as are offered by homoeopathists? Whilst these arguments have some force we cannot, I believe, condone a doctor's manipulation of an autonomous patient's choice by concealing information from her. But doctors can hardly disregard a patient's preference for the 'standard plus' treatment on the grounds that it is unsafe since, as we have observed, they are willing to submit half their patients to it.

Finally, doctors withhold information about alternative treatments in the course of ordinary therapy with the sole purpose of benefiting their individual patient and so are merely paternalistic. But doctors using the Zellen method of pre-randomisation conceal from their patients the existence of an alternative treatment to the 'standard' treatment largely to ensure satisfactory recruitment to an RCT which they hope may advance knowledge and so help future patients. For them, the requirement of informed consent is, as one doctor has frankly put it, 'an unfortunate obstacle to scientific progress'[29]. But in thus manipulating the patient's choice, not in her own but in other patients' interests (which could conflict with her interests), they use their patient, as Kantians would argue, as a 'mere means' to their ends. Yet supporters of the Zellen method of pre-randomisation do not see how this can be wrong since, they claim, they are giving their patient what they believe to be the best treatment. We can only conclude that their account of the doctor's duty is dangerously deficient. A doctor has, as they rightly point out, a duty to give his patient what he believes to be the better treatment or at least not to put her at risk of receiving what he already knows is the worse treatment. But he must also refrain from doing anything to his patient which is not for her benefit, unless he first obtains her informed consent. This, however, entails a role for informed consent in making RCTs permissible which requires the abandonment of the paternalistic conception of the doctor–patient relationship.

Acknowledgement

I am grateful to Dr A. R. Jonckheere of University College London for reading and commenting on earlier drafts of this chapter.

Notes and references

1. Arthur Schafer, 'The Ethics of the Randomized Clinical Trial', *The New England Journal of Medicine*, 307 (1982) p. 720; C. Fried 'Medical Experimentation: Personal Integrity and Social Policy', in A. G. Bearn, D. A. K. Black and H. H. Hiatt (eds), *Clinical Studies*, Vol. 5. (New York: Elsevier, 1974); I. Kennedy 'Consent and Randomized Controlled Trials', in his *Treat Me Right* (Oxford: Clarendon Press, 1988) pp. 219–20, 222.

2. Michael Baum, in 'The Ethics of Clinical Research' (the preceding chapter of this volume, argues that it is not only permissible but obligatory to enter patients into RCTs, since any possible disadvantage to an individual patient is quite outweighed by the advantage for future patients of obtaining knowledge that will combat disease. Indeed for him it is the 'scientific necessity' of RCTs, as the only means of obtaining the requisite knowledge, which makes them morally obligatory. He maintains, however, that, except where there are therapeutic reasons against it, not seeking the patient's consent is morally wrong, since it violates her autonomy.

3. I assume that it would, in these circumstances, be wrong even to *recommend* patients to enter an RCT since doctors have a duty to offer the best advice to patients. It may be objected that patients can make up their own minds despite such a recommendation. But as Schafer, Kennedy and others point out, sick patients tend to defer submissively to their doctor's advice and hence may well be incapable of giving a proper informed consent.

4. Kennedy, 'Consent', p. 220.

5. Ibid., p. 219.

6. Fried, 'Medical Experimentation'.

7. Schafer 'The Ethics', p, 720.

8. Baum, 'The Ethics'.

9. Sir Austin Bradford Hill is perhaps the most famous, see his *Principles of Medical Statistics*, (London: *The Lancet*, 1971) pp. 245–7.

10. I discuss the appropriateness of using the notion of rights in this context later in the chapter.

11. Hill, *Principles*, pp. 245–7.

12. A form of expression frequently used by researchers, see Schafer, 'The Ethics', p. 722.

13. R. J. Levine, 'Ethical Issues in Clinical Trials', in V. Mike and K. Stanley (eds), *Statistics in Medical Research* (New York: John Wiley, 1982) p. 164–5.

14. See D. Vere, 'Problems in Controlled Trials,' *Journal of Medical Ethics*, vol. 9 (1983) pp. 85–9, cited by Peter Byrne in his helpful article 'Medical Research and the Human Subject', in Callahan and G. R. Dunstan (eds), *Biomedical Ethics: An Anglo-American Dialogue* (New York: New York Academy of Sciences, 1988) p 151.

15. Levine 'Ethical Issues', p. 165, and again in R. J. Levine, 'Protection of Human Subjects of Biomedical Research in the United States' in Callahan and Dunstan (eds), *Biomedical Ethics*, p. 137. Here again Levine misleadingly associates the null hypothesis with 'the judgement that two treatments are potentially medically equivalent in terms of such gross outcome measures as life expectancy and probability of recurrence of cancer'.

16. J. P. Gilbert, 'Statistics and Ethics in Surgery and Anesthesia' in 'A Symposium on Medical Research: Statistics and Ethics', *Science*, vol. 198 (1977) p. 687.

17. Baum, 'The Ethics'.

18. Schafer 'The Ethics', p. 723.

19. V. Herbert, 'Acquiring New Information While Retaining Old Ethics', *Science*, vol. 198 (1977).
20. Hill, *Principles*, pp. 245–7.
21. See W. Silverman, *Human Experimentation*, (Oxford: Oxford Medical Publications, 1985) p. 116.
22. J. B. Kadane, 'Progress Toward a More Ethical Method for Clinical Trials', *Journal of Medicine and Philosophy*, vol. 11 (1986), p. 385–405.
23. A helpful, not too mathematical, account of the Bayesian principles is: L. D. Phillips, *Bayesian Statistics for Social Scientists* (London: Nelson, 1973).
24. For an analysis of Kant's notion of 'using someone merely as a means to an end', see my 'Abortion, Embryo Research and Foetal Transplantation: Their Moral Interrelationships', in Peter Byrne (ed.), *Medicine, Medical Ethics and the Value of Life*, (Chichester, John Wiley, 1990) pp. 51–8.
25. For a helpful account of the two different conceptions of rights, see L. W. Sumner, *The Moral Foundation of Rights* (Oxford: Clarendon Press, 1989) pp. 93–111.
26. J. Tobias, 'Informed Consent and Controlled Trials' *Lancet*, vol. ii (1988) p. 1194; see also Baum, 'The Ethics'.
27. M. Zelen, 'A New Design for Randomised Clinical Trials', *New England Journal of Medicine*, vol. 300 (19) pp. 1242–5. Helpful articles on the Zelen method are: D. Anbar, 'The Relative Efficiency of a Zelen's Prerandomization Design for Clinical Trials', vol. 39 (1983) pp. 711–8; and D. Marquis 'An Argument That All Prerandomized Clinical Trials Are Unethical', *Journal of Medicine and Philosophy*, vol. 11 (1986) pp. 367–85.
28. Here patients who are prerandomised to the standard treatment are also given the option of receiving the alternative treatment.
29. Tobias, 'Informed Consent'.

Some ethical aspects of current fetal usage in transplantation

Peter McCullagh

Whilst discussion of the ethical implications of novel therapeutic proposals will often need to include hypothetical and projected developments, there can be no substitute for a thorough familiarity with any relevant information that is already available. As regards the use of the human fetus as a donor of tissues and organs for therapeutic transplantation, this has been actively considered, frequently advocated and intermittently practised for several decades.[1]

The fetal tissues that have been transplanted in attempts to compensate for impaired function of recipient organs include the thymus and parathyroid glands, cells from the liver and pancreas and, most recently, cells from the brain. In a related development, anencephalic infants, either intentionally delivered before term or born after a full period of gestation, have been identified as candidate donors of kidneys and hearts.

If the scientific literature is taken as an accurate and comprehensive guide to current fetal tissue transplantation practice (this assumes that significant initiatives in research or therapy are not underway without accompanying publication), the overall picture of usage of fetal organs and tissues in 1989 may be summarised as follows. Clinical use of fetal thymus and liver cells continues in very few centres, most notably at Lyon.[2] Therapeutic use of fetal pancreatic islet transplantation has failed to become established after trials in many centres. The results of this procedure have been regularly recorded and reviewed in the *Pancreas and Islet Trans-*

plant Registry Report prepared on behalf of the Transplantation Society by the Department of Surgery of the University of Minnesota. Thus, the most recent report to have considered transplantation of islets observed:

> Clinical attempts at transplantation of free grafts of pancreatic islet tissue, derived from either human fetal pancreas or from dispersed adult human pancreas, have been unsuccessful in terms of establishing a permanent normoglycemic insulin-independent state. Thus, only the clinical experience with pancreas transplantation is emphasized in this report.[3]

The next *Transplant Registry Report*, while noting that 220 cases of pancreas transplantation had been documented in the preceding 10 months, made no mention of any use of islet transplantation, even omitting the subject from its title.[4] Clinical application of fetal brain cell transplantation, the most recent variant, is currently being undertaken in Sweden and, more frequently, in the UK.

To summarise the current position, with the exception of fetal brain cell usage, reported clinical recourse to most forms of fetal tissue transplantation has become much less frequent during the past decade. A summary of earlier practice in relation to the use of thymus and pancreatic islets illustrates this trend.[5] As the use of fetal brain cells in clinical transplantation is the most recently introduced and also the most intensively discussed, and as it appears to be the only form of fetal tissue transplantation currently practised in the UK, it is appropriate to use it as an example for discussion of the issues raised by this type of treatment.

It is easy, when considering the ethical aspects of any new medical procedure, to overlook the reality that some of the most significant of these will inevitably be shared with other procedures. Fetal brain cell transplantation is no exception. It may be a consequence of the increasing popularity of 'bioethical issues' as subjects for discussion in the mass media, especially television, that the most specific features of any situation tend to attract exclusive attention while little attempt is made to place the subject in its wider context. It certainly seems that the approach of fastening on to those aspects of the subject that are peculiar to it, at the expense of others, has often been adopted in consideration of fetal usage in transplantation. In order to avoid this tendency, I intend to discuss considerably broader ethical aspects. They will relate to:

- the communication of results and prospects
- donor procurement
- consistency in treatment of human subjects
- exposure of recipients to risk
- manipulation of potential recipients and their families
- conflict of interests between donors and recipients as transplantation techniques are refined.

Before discussing any of these specifically ethical topics it is appropriate to emphasise the importance, during their consideration, of familiarity with the technical aspects of the subject.

The relevance of any ethical examination to clinical practice is dependent upon the accuracy of the data on which it is based

The adage of garbage in garbage out is potentially applicable to any attempt at ethical analysis of a biomedical subject. A discussion that is based on hypothetical situations may be intrinsically logical and consistent in arriving at its conclusions. Such an approach is often of assistance in arriving at decisions on a subject that carries ethical connotations. However, there can be no greater disservice to either science or ethics than to present a discussion based on a mixture of scientific fact, imagination and unscientific commentary as if it were a reasoned ethical analysis. More often than not such 'analyses' do no more than mirror the advocacy favoured by the sources of imperfect data input.

The tendency for ethical examination of biomedical subjects to become divorced from reality may result from the attitude that medical research and ethics can be rigorously separated. On the one hand, the scientific literature relating to many subjects has become increasingly inaccessible to those without current interests in those particular subjects. On the other, there is an increasingly evident tendency of scientists to opt out of participation in ethical commentary on their work and its implications. The rejoinder that one is only undertaking medical research and cannot be expected to deliver an opinion on the ethical status of its consequences has become commonplace. Evidently, it has become a task for the specialist ethicist to distinguish between right and wrong.

What are the technical considerations that must be satisfied before anyone sets out to examine the ethical implications of a projected medical technique? Among them would certainly be an accurate knowledge of the current status of the proposal. Does a procedure work effectively and *reproducibly* achieve the outcome that is claimed? If the outcome has yet to be attained, how feasible does that attainment appear to be? Has the procedure been extensively trialled with negative or highly inconsistent outcomes?

In responding to the preceding type of questions, it is necessary to exercise discrimination regarding the source of any data to be included in the analysis. Have the reports of achievement with the procedure been published in refereed scientific journals, in review articles or in a daily newspaper? It is equally necessary that one be familiar with the context into which the procedure is to be introduced. Are alternative therapeutic procedures available, or under development? How effective are they? Reductionism is becoming belatedly, but deservedly, recognised as a potential hazard in science. It is time that it was similarly recognised in relation to the ethics of science.

Accuracy of the data and validity of the claims advanced for new medical procedures that may be ethically contentious become essential when those procedures are to be assessed within a consequentialist framework. If an anticipated benefit from implementation of a procedure is to be of sufficient magnitude to override countervailing claims based on its unfavourable aspects, it is essential that the claim of a benefit be valid. The legitimacy of any consequentialist analysis which resolves an ethical problem by arguing that an end benefit proportionately outweighs preceding stages is totally at the mercy of the source of claims for the end benefit. If this is unreliable and the result is not as advertised, the argument fails. Furthermore, if it can reasonably be predicted that the benefit will not eventuate, the credibility of the analyst will be impaired.

The ethics of communication

Truth is the most basic ethical question in any scientific communication. This may appear a self-evident and superfluous statement, but current trends in publicisation of all manner of potentially therapeutic procedures unfortunately ensure that it is neither. It may prompt the question, 'Truth. What is that?' immortalised by

Pilate.[6] The answer, in the present context, might appropriately run along the line of another question 'When does hyperbole become untruth?' All too often, it seems, from the comments that have been attributed to some of the medical personnel responsible for undertaking and promoting fetal brain cell transplantation as a therapeutic mode. As an example of an approach to presentation of the results of a highly experimental, ethically contentious and potentially dangerous new form of therapy, consider the following newspaper headlines employed when an English neurosurgical group based in Smethwick, elected to use the lay press as a primary site of publication for results of the transplantation of fetal brain cells to patients with Parkinsonism. 'My story, by brain transplant wife', 'I watched mother come out of hell' and 'New life plan by brain transplant woman'. All appeared within days of the operations. Predictably, presentations of this ilk elicited some adverse responses which, in their turn brought a rejoinder from the leader of the neurosurgical team 'Brain transplant pioneers vow to carry on'.[7] In contrast, a Swedish neurosurgical team from the University of Lund adopted the more conventional approach of waiting for 6 months and an independent assessment before communicating the results of similar surgical procedures in a medical journal. Their conclusion that, 'no improvements of therapeutic value to the patients have been observed up to 6 months postoperatively' were based on operations undertaken at a similar time to their English counterparts.[8]

It is difficult to believe that promotion of a proposal in the media does not influence attitudes towards it. It is likely that the source of these influences may soon pass from memory, by which time the proposition that a nominated procedure produces a certain outcome may well grade into the 'it is widely known' category. It is very unlikely that retraction of a published medical claim on the grounds of hyperbole (a rare event in any case) would have any effect in counteracting the headline of the previous day.

The influence of donor procurement on the ethics of fetal brain cell transplantation

Unless one subscribes to the view that abortion ceased to have any ethical dimensions in the UK after 1967, it is appropriate to recognise that its role as the mainstay for acquisition of human fetal tissues will inevitably have some bearing on ethical assessment of programmes for fetal tissue transplantation. While there are likely to be a range of opinions regarding the impact of each event on the ethical status of the other, there are some associations that are clearly verifiable from examination of the technical aspects of transplantation. A prime example of these is the influence that selection of abortion technique will exert on the subsequent usefulness of any fetal tissue for transplantation. One way in which this association arises relates to the close correlation that exists between the technique selected and the interval that will, in consequence, be likely to elapse between fetal death and availability of the body for tissue collection. During this interval in which fetal organs remain deprived of blood supply and oxygen, at maternal body temperature, they are subject to rapid deterioration. It may be inferred that the state of preservation of a transplant, and hence the success of its subsequent transfer to a recipient patient, will be strongly affected by the technique of abortion used.

Inferences of an association between the technique used to terminate a pregnancy and the success of subsequent fetal tissue transplantation are supported by clinical outcomes. Laboratory studies have shown, for example, that human fetal pancreatic islet survival was greatly impaired if tissue was obtained after prostaglandin-induced abortion rather than after hysterotomy.[9,10]. Use of tissue from prostaglandin-induced termination has probably contributed significantly to the failure of fetal pancreatic islet transplantation to gain acceptance as a procedure to alleviate diabetes. Tissues are likely to sustain damage during the period of warm ischaemia elapsing between fetal death and expulsion from the uterus. As already mentioned, recent reviews of the use of pancreatic transplantation as an alternative form of management of diabetes provide a good indication of the extent to which fetal islet transplantation has now been abandoned.

The extent of cellular survival required in a fetal specimen in order to achieve successful growth of some of its constituent cells *in vitro* is likely to be substantially less than that required for survival of the same specimen after transplantation to a recipient patient. Yet, the operators of the Royal Marsden Hospital Fetal Tissue Bank indicated that, 'tissue cultures using organs obtained from fetuses after a medical induction produce only a limited yield of viable cells. It therefore became apparent in the early 1970s that if the Bank were to continue to meet its commitments, some other source of tissue would have to be found'.[11] The state of preservation of any tissue recovered from an aborted fetus, in regard to its suitability for use in transplantation, will vary not only with the technique of abortion but also with the sensitivity to deprivation of oxygen of the specific tissue which is required. The period for which an organ or tissue can remain capable of survival after oxygen deprivation at body temperature (warm ischaemia) varies widely. Two of the longest surviving types of cells are those found in skin and connective tissue which often form the basis for tissue cultures. In contrast, brain cells survive for the shortest period. When an abortion technique that kills the fetus *in utero* is selected, a particularly relevant influence on the capacity of fetal tissue for survival between fetal death and expulsion from the uterus (when the tissue can be recovered) is the enforced maintenance of the dead fetus at $37°C$, the maternal body temperature. Whereas the body temperature of a 'conventional' dead subject rapidly decreases after death, that of the fetus *in utero* does not. Consequently, deterioration of tissues occurs at an unprecedented rate.

Apart from substantially influencing the state of preservation in which various fetal tissues are likely to be recovered, the technique of abortion will affect the usefulness of fetal tissues for transplantation in another way. The technique that is selected will determine the likelihood with which particular types of tissue can be identified and recovered, irrespective of their condition at that time. For instance, there are major limitations to the facility and frequency with which some organs can be identified and recovered following suction evacuation of the uterus. As this technique entails dismemberment of the fetal body by suction, physically softer tissues are liable to be delivered in a much more disrupted form than are more firmly structured parts such as limbs. This may outweigh the apparent advantage of suction evacuation as a means of providing fetal tissues that have not been subject to warm ischaemia. (As the fetus remains alive until suction is initiated to dismember it and evacuate the proceeds, tissues may be available in a very fresh state.) To quantify the impact of selection of suction evacuation as a means of abortion on relative success rate of tissue recovery, the workers at the Marsden Fetal Tissue Bank reported that, whereas they could recover identifiable upper and lower limbs in 74% and 61% of cases respectively, the comparable frequencies for the brain and adrenal gland were 8% and 1%.[12]

The implications of these influences of abortion technique on the frequency of recovery of different tissues and on their suitability, when recovered, for subsequent transplantation are very important in determining the degree of compatibility between different techniques and the transfer of specific tissue types. The selection of abortion technique to be used in any case would normally be influenced by a number of factors. These could include the age of the fetus, the geographical location of the event and the time and finances available to the mother (out-patient versus in-patient procedure). All of these considerations will then, indirectly, influence the availability and suitability for transplantation of any specific type of tissue from the aborted fetus.

A factor which will be controlled quite independently, but which will have a major impact on fetal utility as a transplant donor in the individual case, will be the gestational age of the fetus. Different transplant regimes have quite distinct requirements in this respect. Whereas fetal pancreas donors should be as mature as the constraints of local abortion practice permit (perhaps 16–18 weeks in the UK), fetal brain cells for use in the treatment of Parkinsonism are thought to be at their best as early as 9 weeks. Fetal liver, it is believed, should be obtained from donors of less than 12 weeks in order to minimise graft-versus-host disease. It is clearly uninformative and misleading, if not mischievious, when advocating the use of fetal tissue in transplantation, to remain under the cover afforded by ignoring the specific requirements of different types of transplant and the incompatibilities generated by them.

Attempts to raise the possibility that any influences operating between the practice of abortion and fetal brain transplantation may be bidirectional often evoke the accusation that one is postulating the unthinkable – that abortions will be undertaken in order to procure fetal tissue for transplantation. There are, however, other ways in which vigorous promotion of techniques such as fetal brain cell transplantation may affect abortion practice. Influences in either direction may be considered as operating both at the level of individual cases and at that of general trends. The specific characteristics that have been mentioned relating to abortion techniques and use of different tissues provide examples of the former. A general influence of trends in abortion practice on the development of fetal tissue transplantation has unquestionably been the facilitating effect of location of a greatly increased number of abortions in the sterile operating theatres of hospitals, with the result that tissue may be collected in a condition conducive to its subsequent transplantation. Serious development of attempts at fetal tissue transplantation based on the limited availability of fetuses from mothers with life-threatening illnesses in hospitals before 1967 would have been out of the question. In what ways, and to what extent, may widespread success with techniques such as fetal brain cell transplantation, or even the widespread *perception* of such success, influence the evolution of abortion practice? At least two pathways of influence appear likely to develop. In the first place, the attachment to abortion of a socially laudable objective, namely the saving or prolonging of life by means of transplants, is likely to influence positively both the acceptance and the continuation of the practice. The original acceptance of ready availability of abortion appears often to have been based on the proposition that this provided a temporary measure of value until the effective application of contraceptive measures. As such, there is little doubt that many of those supporting abortion law reform two or three decades ago regarded it as an issue which would disappear. However, the creation of an ongoing outlet for therapeutic use of the by-products of abortion would be likely to act as a powerful incentive for the permanent entrenchment of the practice at least at existing levels. The analogy of the relationship between capital punishment and proposals for use of condemned criminals in medical research bears many similarities. It is notable that advocacy of the use of condemned subjects as the objects of research three decades ago[13] evoked total resistance from opponents of capital punishment. The basis for this opposition was surely the anticipation that development of beneficial end uses for executed individuals would militate against any phasing out of the practice of capital punishment.

A second way in which adoption of programmes of fetal brain cell transplantation may, imperceptibly, influence abortion practice could be through gradual modifications of that practice in order to provide tissue with the properties most suited to the end use. Given the fact that tissues produced by some types of abortion are unsuitable for transplantation, it may not be too implausible to suggest that trends in relative popularity of different techniques may gradually come to reflect transplantation requirements.

This point can best be illustrated by considering a specific situation such as the example, already mentioned, of fetal brain cell transplantation for the treatment of Parkinsonism. In this instance, the tissue required is not the whole, or even a major portion, of the brain. The tissue to be transferred, namely the substantia nigra, contains at most several thousand cells with the required property of dopamine production (whereas the total brain cell content, even in the prospective fetal donor, would be in the millions). Fetuses obtained in the course of a prostaglandin or prostaglandin and saline abortion would almost invariably have been dead for sufficient time to ensure that the fetal brain was no longer of value for transplantation. Consequently, it would be necessary to use fetuses obtained as a result of suction evacuation of the uterus or by hysterotomy. Both approaches have been used in investigation of recovery of the substantia nigra.

As indicated already in considering the success rate of recovery of identifiable portions of different organs following suction abortion, brain tissue can be confidently recognised in only a minority of cases. Isolation of the specifically required small portion of the brain would be a difficult and slow procedure. The risk of its contamination with other cell types, and the attendant hazard of this for the transplant recipient, as discussed later, could be substantial. Nevertheless, isolation of the substantia nigra from the remains of disrupted fetuses has been achieved. It remains unanswered whether this technique is likely to be successfully scaled up to provide a reliable way of retrieving sufficient uncontaminated tissue of the appropriate type required to underpin a clinical transplantation programme. Hysterotomy and also removal of the intact fetus through the dilated cervix, as practised in one Swedish clinic as a means of obtaining fetal brain tissue for transplantation, are likely to provide a fetus that is alive, or very recently dead, from which the substantia nigra can be accurately recovered free from contamination. Without doubt such tissue would be more suitable for transplantation. However, there is no doubt that these abortion techniques would rarely be indicated on obstetric grounds in the first trimester of pregnancy, the gestational age most suitable for transplantation.

To formulate any analysis of the possible impact of a procedure such as fetal brain cell transplantation were it to become successful (or even to be perceived as such) without taking account of specifics such as these would be a worthless exercise. For example, a procedure such as recovery of fragments of substantia nigra from a suction-disrupted fetus might be effective in providing limited quantities of tissue for transplantation as a research procedure but become inadequate if the availability of transplantation were to be extended to the full range of patients seeking this form of treatment. Interestingly, an excellent illustration of this point has become available during the preparation of this article. The initial fetal brain cell transplantations undertaken at the Midland Centre for Neurosurgery and Neurology utilised tissue fragments isolated from 'conventional' first trimester suction abortions. As implied above, the identification and extraction of uncontaminated substantia nigra cells from these fragments is likely to be a difficult procedure not readily susceptible to being scaled up. Hence, it was not surprising to find, a year after the first operations, the Midland neurosurgical group reporting that they 'experienced difficulty in gathering and identifying donor tissue for transplantation'.[14] As a result, it was revealed that 'rather than first trimester abortion material we now use older fetuses from 12 to 18 weeks gestation. These larger fetuses are delivered intact and dissection results in bigger cell blocks.' This report (April 1989) indicating as it does a concern with the technical detail of the procurement of the fetal tissue to be used in transplantation, provides an interesting contrast with the previous disavowal by its authors, in May 1988, of any knowledge of such matters: 'The tissue I used was collected routinely. It was not obtained specially for me. I do not know what method was used but it was obtained in the usual way.'[15]

The disclosure by Hitchcock et al. of abandonment of suction-disrupted fetuses in favour of subjects removed intact from the uterus, albeit at an older gestational age, was evoked in response to a Swedish report of a different response to an identical difficulty. The Swedish report stated that, 'with the techniques for first-trimester abortion then in use damage to the fetal brain cells rendered them unsuitable for transplantation'.[16] Its solution to this problem was not to vary the age at which fetuses were to be used but to modify the technique of abortion in the first trimester. With the patient under general anaesthesia, a suction tube was introduced into the uterus and approximated to the fetus under ultrasonic guidance. The application of suction for a limited period was then reported to result in the removal of fragments of the fetal body uncontaminated by placental tissue.

In responding to this suggestion, Hitchcock et al. made the point that modification of abortion technique in order to improve collection of fetal tissue was prohibited by the Peel code in the UK.[17]

However, their report in its turn, led to a call from a London neurologist for modifying existing abortion techniques in order to optimise conditions for fetal tissue collection.[18]

The ethics of inconsistent treatment of human subjects

Consistency is generally considered to be an essential feature of an ethical approach to any subject. When ethical treatment of organ donors and potential organ donors is considered, the even-handed application of criteria for diagnosis of death is of prime importance. To ignore this point is to endorse the unequal and unfair application of donor selection criteria to different subjects to suit the convenience of the practitioner before any interest of the subject who is to provide tissue.

The criteria that have been framed to define brain death meet several objectives. Originally, they afforded a means of delineating consistent guidelines for the withdrawal of resuscitative measures from subjects incapable of benefiting from them. Subsequently, they provided consistent guidance in identifying donors suitable as a source of transplantable tissues. Finally, and most importantly, the very consistency of the criteria for diagnosis of brain death, irrespective of the identity, age or social status of the subject, conveyed an impression of fairness that served to engender community confidence in transplantation. Any semblance of consistency in treatment of donor subjects is likely to be eroded once one elects to include fetal subjects in the net.

Whether the criteria for diagnosis of death become an issue in relation to fetal usage in tissue donation will be determined by the specific use envisaged for the tissue. If this is such that termination can be accomplished by fetal dismemberment within the uterus, without prejudice to the success of usage, the question of diagnosis of death does not arise in relation to removal of tissue from the fetus. On the other hand, should there be specific requirements relating to viability of fetal tissue, to its identification or to its preparation in an uncontaminated state, then delivery of the donor by hysterotomy or cervical dilatation in an intact and possibly living state will be indicated. Published results from one Scandinavian group suggest that a frequency of 50% or more live births could be expected when hysterotomy is undertaken.[19] In this context, it is apparent that the decision of Hitchcock *et al.*, referred to above, to adopt the use of second trimester fetuses delivered intact for collection of substantia nigra cells places the issue of diagnosis of fetal death squarely on the agenda.

Whereas the diagnosis of brain death cannot legitimately be made in the postnatal subject unless the body temperature of the subject exceeds 35°C, this requirement has failed to attract even lip service on occasions when fetuses *ex utero* have been used in experimentation.[20]. The purpose underlying the requirement is that lowering of body temperature by 5–10°C may result in reversible slowing or weakening of the heartbeat to such an extent as to render it no longer detectable. The effect of lowered body temperature on detectability of heart action is accentuated by the incapacity of the fetus *ex utero* to maintain body temperature. In effect, once the fetus is removed from the uterus it exhibits poikilothermia, that is the temperature of its body rapidly equilibrates with that of its surroundings. It requires no more than to recall historical precedent to make the point that the fetus *ex utero* has been incorporated in experimental procedures without regard for its vital status.[21]

Quite apart from the confounding effects of hypothermia, the near impossibility of making an accurate diagnosis of fetal death, because of the difficulty of interpreting neurological signs, is well documented. Diagnosis of brain death, even in the neonate, is an unreliable procedure as reflected in the most recent adjudication on this subject by the Ethics Committee of the Child Neurology Society (US). This committee concluded 'that there were no valid criteria for determining brain death in newborn infants'.[22] Diagnosis in the fetus *ex utero* is more difficult.

This difficulty is said to have induced the Loma Linda cardiac transplantation team to select a chimpanzee rather than a human donor initially for cardiac transplantation and subsequently to attempt to establish the use of anencephalic infants (both singularly unsuccessful ventures at the time of writing). The well-recognised difficulty of determining the irreversiblity required for brain death diagnosis in the fetus produced a controversy in France in the early 1980s with a prominent paediatric neurologist challenging the validity of protocols for diagnosis of fetal death.[23]

The practical encumbrances introduced into transplantation of fetal tissues by the niceties of consistent diagnosis of death revolve around the likelihood that maintenance of the candidate donor's body temperature above 35°C during the terminal stages will assuredly prejudice the condition of any transplantable tissues removed *post mortem*. However, if cooling of the moribund subject is undertaken to reduce tissue damage as the blood supply fails, the diagnosis of cessation of cardiac action is likely to become valueless.

From a consequentialist viewpoint, it may be that any measure which carries the risk of reducing public confidence in the fairness, objectivity and consistency of criteria selected for diagnosis of death in organ donors will ultimately undermine community support for clinical transplantation.

To what extent is it ethical to inflict risk upon a patient?

The extent of possible risk to the recipient of a fetal tissue transplant varies enormously with the nature of the tissue to be transplanted. Once again, any assessment of the ethics of the situation is completely dependent upon the specific details of the situation. At one extreme, fetal pancreas transplantation is, to quote Professor Roy Calne of Cambridge: 'experimental research with no benefit to the patient. The surgery is minor and quite safe. About 100 have been performed to date but not one has done any good'.[24] In practice, it has entailed the implantation, usually in a subcutaneous location, of small pieces of tissue that, on the basis of experience, produce neither harmful nor beneficial effects on the recipient. In contrast, transplantation of fetal liver cells to children with immunodeficiency diseases carries the risk of producing a lethal graft-versus-host disease.

The transplantation of fetal substantia nigra to the caudate nucleus, deep within the brain, of patients suffering from Parkinsonism is arguably the most invasive procedure ever introduced into clinical medicine. Whereas, in the case of fetal pancreas transplantation the major risk is that there will be no beneficial effect on the recipient's diabetes, there would appear to be a substantial unexcluded risk that the implantation of foreign tissues in a location within the brain, that would preclude their subsequent removal, may worsen the recipient's condition. At least two specific causes for concern are evident in relation to fetal brain cell transplantation. In the first place, the inadvertent contamination of the tissue to be transferred with non-brain cells may result in the growth of unwanted masses of non-neural tissue in an irretrievable location in the recipient's brain. In particular, the capacity of fetal fibroblasts to proliferate should be a cause for concern. It is possible that these cells could be present as contaminants in the transplant if it was selected from the pot-pourri of tissues provided by vacuum extraction. The minimal technical details provided up to the time of writing about the British brain cell transplantation project imply that substantially more brain tissue than the substantia nigra was transferred. Even if the transplanted tissue is composed exclusively of brain cells, the near certainty that it will ultimately be subject to immunological rejection raises the possibility of production of an area of inflammation deep within the brain that may have undesired functional effects. It is quite predictable that any of these deleterious effects would be likely to be delayed in onset. In view of the prolonged course of rejection of foreign, non-tumour cells after their experimental placement in the brain, these effects might not become evident until more than one or two years after surgery.

When does patient manipulation become an ethical concern?

As soon as the media develop an interest in a medical procedure, particular care is required on the part of medical attendants if exploitation of patients, prospective patients and their families is to be avoided. The extent to which this becomes a problem is dependent upon the specific nature of the procedure. That a subject leaves hospital several days after a successful haemorrhoidectomy is unlikely to attract the media. That the same subject comes home carrying a fetal brain cell transplant is certain to do so. Clinical transplantation has historically held a fascination for the media. However, from the earliest days of the first heart transplants in the late 1960s, some of the transplanters have found the media attention as irresistible as the media has found the subject of transplantation. Whereas the traditional practice in medicine is that evaluation of any new procedure has been the responsibility of one's peers in response to its publication in a technical journal, this has of late been short-circuited by a process of acclamation by the media. In the process, one of the most valuable safeguards imposed by the original system, namely that potential patients and their families would not be exposed to unjustifiably optimistic promotion of the merits of new therapies, has been forgone. With the removal of this restraint, the possibility of inadequately informed advocacy on behalf of particular therapies and the personnel developing them by potential consumers/beneficiaries becomes very real. The remaining restraint on manipulation of specific groups of patients by the media rests with the medical personnel involved. When, as happened with some members of the Midland neurosurgical group, fetal brain cell transplantation was touted as being a possible treatment for a range of degenerative neurological diseases apart from Parkinsonism, it is inevitable that community pressure for its promotion will be generated. The impact of statements such as the following on a large number of gullible potential patients could hardly be other than unfortunate. A member of the neurosurgical team opined that: 'There's a likelihood that if this does prove successful in improving not only the standard but the duration of life, it will be applied to other chronic diseases of the nervous system'. He added that 'these would be degenerative types of disorders, such as Alzheimer's disease and Huntington's chorea'.[25]

Conflicts between the interests of donor and recipient

Awareness of potential conflicts between the interests of organ donors and recipients has influenced the practice of clinical transplantation since its inception. This has been recognised in the conventional adult donor situation by the separation imposed between medical personnel responsible for the care of donor and of recipient. Within this framework, considerable modification of donor management has been introduced in order to improve the prospects of success of the transplantation procedure. Whereas the earliest recipients were transported to the location of the potential donor in order to minimise infliction of inconvenience on the latter, the donor is now invariably transported to the prospective recipient. Originally, donors were classified as such on the basis that irreversible brain damage had occurred and any further attempts at resuscitation would be unproductive intrusions on the patient. However, the regular practice now is to apply to the prospective donor those resuscitative procedures, previously withheld because of lack of benefit, with the new objective of improving the quality of the organs to be removed and, in consequence, the prospects of the recipient. Whereas removal of organs for transplantation formerly occurred only after cessation of cardiac action, it now commonly takes place in anticipation of this event. Interestingly, all of these modifications in donor management have occurred without the necessity for any substantial amendment of the principles underlying the subject.

If the precedent of transplantation of organs from *adult* donors is any guide, pressure to modify the treatment accorded donors in the interests of the recipient can achieve substantial changes. It is feasible to foreshadow at least some of the trends which may emerge in association with fetal organ usage. From the point of view of the clinician undertaking such a transplantation procedure, there is clearly a duty of care to achieve the best possible result for the recipient patient. The factors likely to make the largest contribution to this aim relate to the properties of the tissue to be transferred. As indicated above, the technique used for abortion is likely to introduce substantial differences in the efficacy of any resulting fetal tissue for transplantation. These differences may relate to the extent of deterioration that has occurred because of lack of oxygen. They may also reflect the relative success of recovering a specific type of tissue under differing circumstances. The example, mentioned above, of the change in donor gestational age from first to second trimester in order to facilitate recovery of substantia nigra for transplantation to patients with Parkinsonism raises the issue of balance between interests of donor and recipient. This change in procedure by the Midland neurosurgery group has been criticised on the grounds that the older fetal brain tissue appears likely, on the basis of animal experiments, to be much less effective in restoring neurological function to the recipient.[26]

Compounding the legitimate wish of the transplant clinician to have transplantable tissue or organs supplied in the best possible condition is the even more legitimate wish not to harm the recipient. As discussed above, there is no other form of fetal tissue transplantation which is likely to make greater demands upon those collecting the tissue in this respect than will substantia nigra cells. Experience suggests that the pressure already exerted to modify tissue collection procedures for both of these reasons may become considerable if this form of therapy gains popularity. A compounding effect of such a trend may be to necessitate qualitative changes in procedures associated with tissue collection. As already mentioned, a technique that may be quite adequate for the preparation of the limited amount of tissue required to treat an occasional patient may not lend itself to the scaling up necessitated if treatment is to be offered to all who might benefit from it. This may be a most decisive influence when treatment relates to a condition as prevalent as Parkinsonism.

Conclusion

Formulation of ethical decisions in relation to a subject such as fetal brain cell transplantation is not a simple matter of examining one or two selected aspects of the procedure. The range of factors that should influence that decision is at least as broad as the examples given in this article. Examination of each of these aspects requires familiarity with the specific circumstances that relate to it. It is misleading and inaccurate to attempt to evaluate ethical implications without access to accurate technical details. Finally, whilst an assessment of any individual aspect requires attention to detail, it is necessary to consider the outcome of these individual assessments as a whole in reaching a decision about the subject.

Notes and references

1. For a summary of the history of fetal tissue transplantation, see P. McCullagh, *The Fetus as Transplant Donor* (Chichester, John Wiley, 1987) pp. 22–6.
2. J.-L. Touraine, 'European Experience with Fetal Tissue Transplantation in Severe Combined Immunodeficiency', *Birth Defects*, vol. 19 (1983) p. 139.
3. D. E. R. Sutherland and K. C. Moudry, 'Clinical Pancreas and Islet Transplantation', *Transplantation Proceedings*, vol. 19 (1987) no. 1, p. 113.
4. D. E. R. Sutherland and K. C. Moudry, 'Pancreas Transplant Registry Report', *Transplantation Proceedings*, vol. 19 (1987), no. 4, suppl. 4, p. 5.
5. See McCullagh, *The Fetus*, ch. 7.
6. John, ch 18, v. 38.
7. Headlines respectively from: *The Sunday Times*, 17 April 1988, *The Sunday Times*, 1 May 1988, *Birmingham Sunday Mercury*, 26 June 1988, and *The Sunday Times*, 5 June 1988.
8. O. Lindvall *et al.* (19 other authors from 6 clinics) 'Fetal Dopamine-rich Mesencephalic Grafts in Parkinson's Disease', *Lancet*, vol ii (1988) p. 1483.
9. T. Otonkoski, *et al.* 'Yield and Functional Integrity of Islet-like Cell Clusters in Culture of Human Fetal Pancreata from Hysterotomy, Mechanical and Prostaglandin-induced Abortions,' *Diabetologia*, vol. 29 (1986) p. 579A.
10. S. Sandler *et al.* 'Tissue Culture of Human Fetal Pancreas. Effects of Human Serum on Development and Endocrine Function of Isletlike Cell Clusters', *Diabetes*, vol. 36 (1987) p. 1401.

11. S. D. Lawler, 'Conception and Development of the Fetal Tissue Bank', *Journal of Clinical Pathology*, vol. 34 (1981) p. 240.
12. B. Markowski and S. D. Lawler, 'Use of Early Fetal Tissues Obtained from Suction Termination of Pregnancy', *Lancet*, vol. i (1977) p. 186.
13. J. Kevorkian, 'Capital Punishment or Capital Gain', *Journal of Criminal Law, Criminology and Police Science*, vol. 50 (1959) p. 50.
14. E. R. Hitchcock *et al.* 'Fetal Brain Tissue', *Lancet*, vol. i (1989) p. 839.
15. *The Observer*, 1 May 1988.
16. B. Gustavii, 'Fetal Brain Transplantation for Parkinson's Disease: Technique for Obtaining Donor Tissue', *Lancet*, vol. i (1989) p. 565.
17. Hitchcock *et al.*, 'Fetal brain tissue', p. 839.
18. S. B. Blunt, 'Fetal Brain Tissue and Parkinson's Disease', *Lancet*, vol. i, (1989) p. 1021.
19. S. Kullander and B. Sunden, 'On the Survival and Metabolism of Normal and Hypothermic Pre-viable Human Foetuses', *Journal of Endocrinology*, vol. 23 (1961) p. 69.
20. A. Like and L Orci, 'Embryogenesis of the Human Pancreatic Islets: A Light and Electron Miscroscopic Study', *Diabetes* vol. 21 (1972) p. 511.
21. P. Adam *et al.*, 'Cerebral Oxidation of Glucose and D-BOH-butyrate by the Isolated Perfused Human Head', *Pediatric Research*, vol. 7 (1973) p. 309.
22. Cited in D. L. Coulter, 'Neurologic Uncertainty in Newborn Intensive Care', *New England Journal of Medicine*, vol. 316 (1987) p. 840.
23. See, *Nature*, vol. 302 (1983) p. 4.
24. *Melbourne Sun*, 19 April 1985.
25. *Huddersfield Daily Examiner*, 2 June 1988.
26. Blunt, 'Fetal Brain Tissue', p. 1021.

Child abuse and the role of the courts in its control

Stephen M. Cretney

Introduction

What is it?

It is comparatively easy to define sex abuse in general terms; and it may be helpful to bear in mind the definition[1] accepted, for example by the DHSS in recent guidance.[2]

> The involvement of dependent, developmentally immature children and adolescents in sexual activities they do not truly comprehend, to which they are unable to give informed consent; or which violate social taboos or family roles.

In many cases, there will be little room for controversy about what constitutes abuse: it is difficult to believe that anyone would wish to exclude penile or digital penetration of a pre-pubertal child by an adult, for example. Yet the judgement may still be a cultural one. A single mother makes love while her daughter is asleep in bed beside her. The daughter, curious about the facts of life, is allowed to look at and touch the lover's penis. Abuse or not? Not, it would seem for the film reviewer writing recently in a quality newspaper;[3] but others may hold different views. How would such an issue be resolved; and what legal consequences – punishment of the adults concerned, decisions about the upbringing of the child, for example – should turn upon this issue?

But can it really be true?

Whatever may be the criteria adopted to define child sexual abuse, there is no doubt that allegations of such behaviour are being made with increasing frequency;[4] but it is not clear either how far abuse in fact occurs, and whether its incidence is increasing. It is, however certainly true that modern European cultural history has been profoundly influenced by the consequences of Freud's renunciation of his earlier belief[5] that premature sexual experience – often with a close relative within the privacy of the family home – was at the root of most or all cases of hysteria. 'Surely', he wrote, 'such perversions against nature are not very probable.'[6] Hence, he came to believe that his patients were merely fantasising on the basis of their own childhood desires; and his recognition of this 'awful truth' was not only significant in the development of the notion of the Oedipus complex, but (on one view[7]) the beginning of psychoanalysis as a science and a therapy.

There is certainly the clearest evidence that child sex abuse may be perpetrated by gifted middle-class people. The experience of Virginia Woolf is well known:[8]

There was a slab outside the dining room door for standing dishes upon. Once when I was very small Gerald Duckworth lifted me onto this, and as I sat there he began to explore my body. I can remember the feel of his hand going under my clothes; going firmly and steadily lower and lower. I remember how I hoped that he would stop; how I stiffened and wriggled as his hand approached my private parts. But it did not stop.

Less well known, but even more striking – if only because abusers so rarely provide such clear evidence against themselves – are the astonishing confessions by Eric Gill, the celebrated artist and calligrapher. He wrote in his diary that he went to his young daughter's bedroom, 'stayed half hour – put p. in her a/hole'. Sadly, Gill seemed unable to give effect to his expressed feeling that 'this must stop'. There is the clearest evidence that his incestuous feelings were frequently consummated. In spite of all this, Gill's biographer records that the daughters 'all grew up, so far as one can see [a possibly important qualification], to be contented and well-adjusted married women'.[9] In contrast, Virginia Woolf was a victim of serious mental illness; but whether her early experiences of abuse by her half-brother played any part in the aetiology of this condition seems likely to remain a matter for speculation.

Law: a blunt instrument?

These two cases might provide material for a fascinating discussion about how they should have been dealt with if the facts had been known; and about the agencies which could most usefully have been involved. But it is an underlying assumption of the present paper that, although the legal system undoubtedly has an important part to play, its role in providing an adequate response to the problem of child abuse is a limited one. A judge with great experience in family cases put one of the problems which lead to this view very clearly.

> The forensic process is reasonably well adapted to determining in broad terms the share of responsibility of each party for an accident at work because the issues are relatively confined in scope, but it is much too clumsy a tool for dissecting the complex inter-actions which go on all the time in a family.[10]

But there is another limitation on the role of the courts which is even more significant in the context of child abuse. Courts embody the judicial power of the state,[11] and they express their conclusions in the form of orders. This notion of compulsion is central to the role of law in our society: if the court makes an order − perhaps even an order directing that a person should cease to be the parent of the child she has given birth to and cared for, and that she should accordingly never be entitled to see that child again − the order must be carried out, and all the coercive apparatus of the state will be available to compel obedience. Many consequences flow from this fact − not least that, to quote the (still unrivalled) prescription for the Family Court given by the Finer Report,[12] the individual involved in court proceedings must 'in the last resort remain the subject of rights, not the object of assistance'. Hence − to give one example significant in the present context − the court must only act on evidence, which those affected have the right to hear and to test.

Limited scope of article

It would be impossible in the space available to analyse comprehensively even the more striking problems which affect the courts' ability to provide an appropriate response in cases of suspected child abuse. I have therefore selected two areas for discussion: the first – apparently technical but in fact raising central policy issues about the role of the legal system – is concerned with the relationship between the criminal and the civil law. The second is a discussion of some of the relevant provisions of the legislation (which will have been enacted as the Children Act 1989* by the time that this article appears in print) dealing with the procedures whereby the state may intervene in family life in cases of suspected abuse. In both cases I have tried to raise issues, rather than to supply answers.

The criminal law and the civil law

Although one can confidently say that most people know that the courts can and do send people to prison, by no means everyone keeps in mind the distinction – basic to the whole outlook of any English lawyer – between the criminal law and the courts which enforce it, on the one hand, and the civil law and the civil courts on the other.

In the field of child abuse – where the abuser will usually (but not always)[13] have committed a criminal offence – civil proceedings will probably be taken in order to decide on the child's future. But the objectives of the criminal and civil law, in this country, are different; and this has consequences which are important and problematic. In essence, although the child's welfare is the primary concern of caring agencies and of the civil law which provides a framework for their work, criminal proceedings (once started) are not and (in my view) could not be primarily concerned with the welfare of the child victim. It is my thesis, therefore, that there may in some cases have to be a choice of priorities between, on the one hand, ensuring the prosecution, conviction and punishment of alleged abusers, and, on the other hand, facilitating the taking of action best suited to promote the welfare of the children concerned; and that at the moment the legal system itself creates obstacles to the resolution of this conflict.

---

*Note: This essay is based on a lecture given in January 1989. It is based on the materials as they were then available.

The role of the criminal law: punishing the guilty

The distinctive feature of criminal proceedings is that they may lead to the punishment of offenders. For example, the Criminal Justice Act 1988 has increased the maximum penalty for the offence of cruelty to children under the age of 16 from two years' to ten years' imprisonment; and it is difficult to open a newspaper without finding calls for more severe sentences to be passed on those guilty of child abuse.

The rationale of punishment

Punishment is usually seen as having at least three objectives: deterrence, retribution and reform. Judicial guidance on sentencing policy heavily emphasises the first two components: custodial sentences are (it is said[14]) necessary to ensure the protection of younger members of society, and to indicate society's abhorrence of behaviour which it finds unacceptable; and as a result of such guidance, child abusers can usually expect to be imprisoned, for periods depending on the nature of the offence.

Where does reform come into the picture? Rule 1 of the Prison Rules still states – notwithstanding changes in informed thinking which now usually prefers to define the objectives of imprisonment more in terms of 'humane containment' – that the purpose of prison training and treatment 'shall be to encourage and assist [convicted prisoners] to lead a good and useful life'.

The experience of imprisonment

It is difficult to believe that many of those imprisoned for offences – and particularly for sexual offences – against children will perceive much encouragement or assistance, or even much humanity, in the conditions in which they are contained. Prisons are violent places in which – notwithstanding the vigilance of the staff – assaults ranging from the murderous stabbing attack to the spillage of urine and faecal matter on to another prisoner's person or food occur frequently. Child molesters are regarded as pariahs by the rest of the prison community,[15] and thus often become targets for other prisoners, who demonstrate by violence that they too share society's abhorrence of sexual deviancy in relation to children.

Not surprisingly, imprisoned child abusers in consequence often ask the authorities to exercise the power under Rule 43 of the

Prison Rules to remove them, 'in their own interests' from association with other prisoners.[16]

The practical effect of such a removal in a normal prison – and it is necessary to use that adjective because in recent years special national and regional units for vulnerable offenders have been created where the regime may be less impoverished – is likely to be that the offender will spend all except one hour of the day confined to a cell. He will thus have ample time to reflect on his own past – and we know that many abusers have themselves been abused as children[17] – and also on the future for himself and his family.

It seems right to emphasise that in many cases the punishment inflicted on child abusers may in practice be severe beyond the comprehension of most of us. But the reader may think – many people certainly do – that the molester has only himself to blame for his predicament; and it is not my purpose to discuss the issue of the punishment of molesters save to make two points in the following section.

Consequences of prosecution

First, whatever our views may be on that issue, it must be right to remember that prosecution and imprisonment of an offender affects not only him, but also the abused victim and the family. In particular, we must take account of the conclusions of some researchers that prosecution in some cases not only serves to break up families in a damaging and destructive way, but that the process also adds to the sense of guilt often experienced by the victim.[18]

Secondly, there is a real danger – and this is a point which deserves to be highlighted – that the objective of punishing offenders will have seriously adverse implications for the legal system's attempts to deal with the consequences of the abuse in the interest of the victim and the other members of the family. It is precisely because conviction of any criminal offence – but particularly one involving something as serious as child abuse – may have such devastating consequences for the accused that the policy of the *criminal* law has traditionally been, and remains today, that the accused be given at his trial the benefit of any reasonable doubt. Moreover, there are procedures (for example, the rules requiring that a suspect must be formally cautioned and reminded of his right to remain silent, and forbidding the giving of inducements – for example, as to the probably advantageous consequences of his making a full disclosure about what has occurred); there are evidential rules (for example, the rule excluding hearsay evidence); and there are procedural principles (for example, the requirement that an accused should be entitled to confront his accuser, and to test the accuser's evidence by cross-examination) which are based on a principle from which, stated in the Introduction, few would dissent. It is that the innocent be protected against unfounded allegations, and that the vulnerable — for example, the parent who has taken a child to hospital for treatment only to find himself in a police cell — will not be pressured into admissions which are in fact untrue.

Precisely where the balance lies between safeguarding the innocent whilst avoiding the scandal of the guilty escaping conviction by reliance on legal technicalities is rightly a matter of constant debate; and, as part of this continuing balancing exercise, the Criminal Justice Act 1988 seeks to remove some obstacles to the conviction of the guilty in child abuse cases — for example, by permitting the use of video links to avoid the child witness being physically confronted by his alleged abuser, and by abolishing the requirement that a child's unsworn evidence necessarily requires corroboration. It is, however, to be noted that the Act does not affect the separate requirement that a judge must warn the jury of the dangers of accepting uncorroborated evidence of sexual offences. But the law lecturer's traditonal jest that the criminal courts are not concerned with the truth, but merely with the question of whether the prosecution has proved the accused's guilt beyond reasonable doubt, still encapsulates the reality of the criminal law.

It is because of rules of the criminal law that no competent lawyer is likely to advise a person whose conduct is being investigated by the police to make any statement which could well form the main — if not the only — evidence against him on a serious criminal charge. This is, of course, likely to bring about a result quite inconsistent with the emphasis now placed by many of those concerned with therapy for the family unit on the need for full disclosure and admission of responsibility as a pre-condition to any useful treatment.

The problem of a potential conflict between he effective investigation of a suspected criminal offence and the policy of ensuring that action be taken which will best protect the child may be all the greater now that so many decisions about whether a child's name should be placed on the 'at risk' register and about the future care of children who are thought to have been abused are taken at case conferences. This is in part because the civil courts have begun to assert the existence of a duty on the part of those initiating and carrying out such procedures to act 'fairly' to an adult suspected of involvement in abuse.[19]

In this context, the requirements of fairness may include informing the adult of the substance of the suspicions against him, and giving him an opportunity to make representations on the matter. Yet if this is done before a decision on any criminal proceedings has been taken, there is an obvious danger that the suspect will subsequently be able to allege that any incriminating statements he makes were obtained by the giving of inducements (for example, that he would be allowed some access to the child if he made a full and complete disclosure).

Joint investigative initiatives

Attempts have been made in some areas to achieve a workable compromise between those conflicting objectives within the framework of the existing law. In particular, there may be interdisciplinary investigative projects which (in the words of the Bexley Joint Investigative Project[20]) are prepared to accept as a 'fundamental principle' that 'the primary aim of joint investigation is the welfare and protection of the child/victim', and that other specific aims, such as arrest and/or prosecution, 'although important', are secondary.

This is no doubt encouraging; although there may be those who feel that the degree of 'importance' to be attached to the aim of prosecuting an offender merits more articulated discussion. (What would be thought appropriate responses in the cases of Messrs Gill and Duckworth, referred to at the beginning of this article, for example?) But at a more mundane level of practice, it is disturbing that, at least until recently, there have been parts of the country in which collaboration – or even mutual understanding – between law enforcement agencies and the caring services have been conspicuously absent. The Butler-Sloss Report[21] considered that, in Cleveland, although the police said that their concern for the welfare of children extended beyond their anxiety to mount a successful prosecution, it was none the less clear that they had concentrated their thoughts on the problems of prosecution, and with conflicts over diagnosis. 'In so doing [the Report concludes] they were losing sight of their wider responsibilities for the interests and welfare of the children involved.'

Policy conflicts remain unresolved

It may be that progress can best be achieved pragmatically and gradually, and in particular by greater interdisciplinary training and communication.[22] But the awkward truth is that there remains a conflict between the policies of criminal and civil evidence and procedure.[23] The Butler-Sloss Report stated under the heading 'Issues for further consideration':

> There is a need to recognise the problems of an abuser who may wish to confess to the abuse but is inhibited from so doing by fear of the consequences. Some consideration might be given in certain circumstances to the wider interests of the child and the family and whether different arrangements might be made in suitable cases for the abusers who admit their guilt, who cooperate with the arrangements for the child and who are prepared to submit themselves to a programme of control.

But how is this to be achieved? There are some[24] who would favour a solution in which a Family Court would first decide on the child's future; and that the criminal court would subsequently be brought in to pass a sentence consistent with the therapeutic programme on which the Family Court had decided. Clearly, however, there would be many problems – some of the more technical of which have been mentioned above – in the way of acceptance of such a solution.

Systematic research needed

It is difficult to escape the conclusion that the various issues (procedures, evidence, sentencing policy) require comprehensive and systematic analysis on an official basis, with a view to producing an acceptable reconciliation, or at least balance, between what are at the moment the conflicting objectives of the civil and criminal justice systems. There are undoubtedly many who would say that the English legal system favours the abuser at the expense of the child victim; but the argument that rules designed to protect the innocent are merely devices whereby advocates can secure acquit-

tals for the manifestly guilty is one which may rightly be regarded
as facile in the country which hanged Timothy Evans.[25]

The civil law – defining the limits of state intervention

The professed objective of the civil law is wholly different from that
of the criminal law: the civil law is, in this context, not concerned
with the punishment of the guilty, but with defining the circumstances in which the state may interfere with the authority which the
law concedes to parents to bring up their children in their own
way. For the civil law, the welfare of the child is the first, albeit not
always the only, consideration.

At the time of writing, the Children Act 1989 is passing through
Parliament. That Act will make a number of important changes in
the law; and its provisions will be considered – necessarily briefly
and inadequately – where appropriate. However, it is right also to
refer, equally briefly, to the provisions of the law which is now in
force and which will remain in force until the provisions of the new
Children Act are implemented – which seems unlikely to be for at
least two years. (It should be noted that citations from the 'Act' are
to the text of the Bill as first introduced; and that consideration is
confined to the fundamental issue of the circumstances and proceedings in which the courts may authorise state intervention into
the family unit – the consideration which is of major importance in
considering the courts' role in case of suspected abuse.)

Place of Safety Orders

The first stage in civil action intended to protect a child will often
be that a social worker applies to a magistrate for a Place of Safety
Order, which authorises the child's removal from home to a 'place
of safety' for a period of up to 28 days. In Cleveland, it appears that
there were no less than 276 applications for such orders between 1
January and 31 July 1987; that 174 orders were made by single
magistrates sitting at home, notwithstanding the fact that the applications could have been made to a full court at the court-house.
The parents had no effective legal redress so long as the orders
were in force; and the Report of the Inquiry into Child Abuse in
Cleveland 1987[26] states that the Child Abuse Consultant in Cleveland Social Services:

believed in a structured and authoritation approach to families where sexual abuse was alleged . . . and saw the place of safety order as the method by which control was gained over that family-. . . . [Some Cleveland social workers] believed that it entitled them to have the child further medically examined and to refuse to allow the parents to have the child examined by doctors of their choice. They believed that they had the right to refuse access or restrict access to parents under the order.[27]

Whatever else may be said about the lessons of Cleveland, it is quite clear that the legal system failed to provide adequate redress for parents whose children were made subject to such orders. Hence, the provisions of the Children Bill which abolish the Place of Safety Order, and substitute an Emergency Protection Order, must be welcomed. Although the subject remains controversial (and the final details had not been settled at the time of writing) it is likely that an Emergency Protection Order will be limited to a maximum duration of 8 days, subject to the possibility of extention for one week and no more. Moreover, the powers conferred by the order are spelt out and, perhaps, restricted – in particular, the local authority will be under a duty to take only such action as it *reasonably required* to safeguard the child's welfare. Finally, provision is to be made for the parents and others to apply after 3 days for the order to be discharged.

The local authority takes over

Whether or not a Place of Safety Order has been made, the local authority may institute care proceedings in the Juvenile Court. As the law now stands, if the court is to make an order, it must be satisfied, first, that one of a number of specified conditions – for example, that the child is being ill-treated – has been proved to exist; secondly, that the child is in need of care and control which he would be unlikely to receive unless an order be made; and thirdly, having regard to the child's welfare, that the making of an order would be appropriate.

The effect of a care order – made, be it noted, by the lowest court in the judicial hierarchy – is drastic. The local authority acquires the powers of a parent over the child, and comes under a duty to keep the child in care notwithstanding any claim by the parent. It is true that the parent may apply for the order to be discharged; it is true that there are some limitations on the scope of the authority's powers – for example, it cannot give the agreement needed to the child's adoption (although it can place the child with a view to adoption); and it is true that – by legislation clearly influenced by the need to comply with the European Convention on Human Rights – a parent whose legal access to the child is formally terminated may apply to the Juvenile Court for access. But, broadly speaking, the effect of a care order is to place the child's future wholly under the control of a local authority.

The alternative route – wardship

There is, as the law now stands, an alternative legal procedure available to a local authority which believes legal intervention to be necessary in the child's interests. This is to make the child a ward of court. There are, for present purposes, three salient characteristics of the wardship jurisdiction. First, it is usually exercised by the judges of the Family Division of the High Court – by the highest rather than the lowest court in the judicial hierarchy. Secondly, no specific 'ground' has to be made out: the principle that the child's welfare is paramount is the golden thread[28] which characterises the jurisdiction; and, specifically, the court has a statutory power to commit a child to the care of a local authority if there are exceptional circumstances making it impracticable or undesirable for him to be under the care of his parents or other individuals.[29] Thirdly – and possibly most significant – all important decisions about the child's future are taken by the court; and the parents have a right to be heard on such issues as whether the child should be placed for adoption. Whereas under a care order all power passes to the local authority, and the procedures for reviewing decisions taken within the scope of that power are not extensive, in wardship all important decisions have to be made on the court's approval. Moreover, the court has a wide range of additional powers to safeguard the child's welfare – for example, to grant injunctions preventing anyone from moving the child.

In recent years, there has been a great increase in recourse to wardship by local authorities: in 1985, 45% of all cases had a local authority element, whereas the comparable figure of 1971 was 2.5%.[30] In part, this may have been because the juvenile court cannot, generally speaking, make an order merely because there is a *risk* of harm to the child – indeed, the Law Commission thought that the absence of forward-looking grounds in care proceedings might account for as many as half of all wardship applications initiated by local authorities.[31] In part, it may have been because the increasing complexity of the evidence requiring to be assessed seemed to make the case suitable for trial by an experienced professional judge; and in part it may have been for the – sometimes associated – reason that it is not always possible to convene benches of lay justices who can give the time necessary for prolonged hearings.

These last two points are highlighted by the Butler-Sloss Report: the number and complexity of the cases in Cleveland in 1987 caused severe difficulties, and ultimately many of the contested cases became wardship applications and it was possible to deal with most of them speedily.[32]

The Children Bill and committal to care

The courts with jurisdiction

What will be the effect of the Children Bill on all this? First, there are to be major changes in care proceedings. Jurisdiction in care proceedings is to be extended to the County Court and High Court. However, the Lord Chancellor has indicated that care proceedings will normally have to be initiated in Magistrate's Courts, and that there will be a power to transfer cases to higher courts if appropriate.

In a refreshingly innovative move, a circuit judge has been appointed to advise the President of the Family Division on the judicial administration necessary to ensure the best possible transition to the new procedures; and the judge will have continuing responsibility for advising on which cases should be heard at which level of court, and for overseeing and co-ordinating the judicial aspects of the operation, including the transfer of cases. It may be that this administrative measure will in practice be found to be amongst the most important of the reforms associated with the new legislation. The procedures for deciding on the appropriateness of a transfer, and the level at which such a decision is to be taken, are obviously crucially important.

Grounds

The substantive law is to be wholly changed: the existing narrow and specific grounds will go; and be replaced by single test. The court may make a care order only if it is satisfied:

(a) that the child concerned has suffered significant harm, or is likely to suffer such harm; and

(b) that the harm, or likelihood of harm, is attributable to

  (i) the standard of care given to the child, or likely to be given to the child if the order were not made, being below that which it would be reasonable to expect the parent of a similar child to give to him; or

  (ii) the child's being beyond parental control.

These changes have been made in response to much thought and consultation. Of course, in many cases the change in the substantive law will not affect the issue. A child who has been subject to anal or vaginal penetration has been ill-treated within the meaning of the existing primary condition; and such a child will undoubtedly have suffered significant harm within the meaning of the proposed legislation. In cases where there are allegations of such a kind, the crucial question will remain the assessment of the evidence; and it is thus essential that cases be allocated to courts which are best able to deal with them. In particular, lay magistrates may not be the best tribunal to assess complex and conflicting medical evidence; and it should be remembered that in Cleveland wardship was used in many cases 'because of the complexity particularly with the considerable volume of medical evidence'.[33]

However, in less extreme cases of alleged poor parenting the new ground will inevitably spawn litigation. The question of whether the evidence is such as to justify a finding of 'likely harm' may cause difficulties, and certainly the need for expert assessment and evidence will be great. Nor does it require much imagination to envisage strenuous legal argument about the aspects of parenting and personality which are properly to be taken into account in deciding on the reasonableness or otherwise of the expectation of standards of care.

Wardship open to all – except local authorities

The third major change to be made by the Bill is much more controversial. Local authorities are to be debarred from using wardship; and the courts' powers to commit a child to care in wardship and other family proceedings are to be much restricted. This proposal is, for a number of reasons, controversial. In particular, the legislation will, for the first time impose a restriction on the right of the authority which has extensive resonsibilities for securing the welfare of children to use whichever legal technique it believes to be most appropriate in the circumstances to achieve that end.

Consider, for example, a case in which a child presents symptoms of disturbances in circumstances such that there is a suspicion – but no clear proof – of sexual abuse. There is, however, evidence that there is a risk in leaving the child without supervision. At the moment, this would for two reasons be a classic case for wardship. First, the court would be well equipped to evaluate all the evidence. Secondly, the court would not be fettered by rules which can operate to exclude relevant evidence.[34] Its primary concern would be whether the evidence indicated that intervention was required in the child's interests, rather than on whether it could be proved that an individual had or had not been guilty of certain behaviour against the child: 'there may be circumstances where the suspicion of sexual abuse ... is such as to lead to the conclusion that it would be an unacceptable risk to the child's welfare to leave him in his previous environment'.[35]

What would happen in such a case under the new code? The answer is that the local authority would not be able to use wardship unless it could obtain leave from the court under the very restrictive provisions set out in the Children Act. On the facts of the hypothetical case, it seems improbable that the authority would be able to satisfy the prescribed conditions. So it would have to start care proceedings. Could it establish the prescribed statutory condition? Possibly wisely, when the Bill was before Parliament the provision (to be found in the Law Commission's draft) dealing with the standard of proof in care proceedings was deleted; but the only honest answer to the question is that would be extremely difficult to be confident that care proceedings would succeed. Even if they did, it seems that the court would not be able to make the complex and detailed order which was made by the High Court in the case on which I have based this example. Again, it seems that the statutory ground set out above could not be available merely because a child was about to be handed over pursuant to a – possible illegal – surrogacy agreement; but under the new law the wardship court could no longer investigate the situation. In the result, it is difficult to avoid the conclusion that the welfare of at least some children is being put at risk.

However, the government has advanced a number of powerful arguments in favour of the decision to restrict the availability of wardship in this way.[36] In particular there is a strong argument from principle (no doubt reinforced by concern that English law should be consistent with the provisions of the European Convention on Human Rights) that defined minimum criteria should be laid down before the state assumes the right to intervene in family life; and that it is wrong to tolerate a situation under which a child may lawfully be removed from his family merely because a court considers that the state could do better for the child than could the family. There are also arguments that local authorities should not be able to undermine the court allocation system to be provided under the Children Act by taking a pre-emptive decision to start wardship proceedings in the High Court.

But these arguments do not satisfy everyone; and the view has been expressed that it would be preferable to await experience of the working of the other reforms effected by the Children Bill so that 'the true scope for a residual power for the courts to assume guardianship over certain children could be determined'[37] in the light of experience. The interpretation of new legislation is a notoriously unpredictable business; and there must always be the risk that experience will show that the draftsman has not anticipated a particular contingency. Where the welfare of children is at risk, the stakes are very high; and it would have been more prudent to reply on the robust application of a statutory directive to the judiciary that wardship be not continued in cases in which the statutory code adequately protects a child's welfare, rather than insisting on the immediate application of a rigid statutory bar to a jurisdiction which historically has demonstrated its utility. We must all hope that events will not show that the Children Act has, in this respect, gone 'too far too fast', by making the legal system less able than in the past to respond appropriately to cases of suspected abuse.

Notes and references

1. Originated by M. D. Schechter and L. Roberge, 'Sexual Exploitation', in R. E. Helfer and C. H. Kempeeds, *Child Abuse and Neglect: The Family and the Community*, (Cambridge, Mass., Ballinger, 1976). This defini-

tion was accepted by the *Report of the Inquiry into Child Abuse in Cleveland*, Cmnd 412 (1988) para. 4.

2. For example, *Diagnosis of Child Sexual Abuse: Guidance for Doctors* (London: HMSO, 1988).

3. See the review by Loretta Loach of the film 'The Good Mother' published in *The Observer*, 5 February 1989. The mother, who fails to win custody of the child against her husband, is said to be a victim of others' moral and legal codes, and evidently exemplifies a punitive climate towards mothers.

4. *Report of the Inquiry into Child Abuse in Cleveland*, para. 6. For the most recently published analysis, see S. J. Creighton and P. Noyes, *Child Abuse Trends in England and Wales 1983–1987* (London, NSPCC, 1989).

5. 'The Aetiology of Hysteria', a paper delivered before the Society for Psychiatry and Neurology, Vienna, 21 April 1896.

6. Letter from Freud to W. Fliess, 1 September 1897, cited in E. Jones, *Sigmund Freud: Life and Work*, vol. 1 (London: Hogarth Press, 1953) p. 292.

7. The whole area is controversial: see for one view J. M. Masson, *Freud, The Assault on Truth, Freud's Suppression of the Seduction Theory* (London: Faber and Faber, 1984).

8. Virginia Woolf, *Moments of Being*, ed. Jeanne Schulkind (1978) p. 69.

9. F. MacCarthy, *Eric Gill* (London: Faber, 1989) p. 135.

10. Ormrod, L. J. (incidentally, perhaps the only High Court judge to have also been a qualified doctor) in *Wachtel* v *Wachtel* [1973] Fam. 72.

11. Contempt of Court Act 1981, s. 19.

12. *Report of the Committee on One-Parent Families*, Cmnd 5629 (1974) para. 4.285.

13. The criminal offences which are most often relevant are summarised in the *Report of the Inquiry into Child Abuse in Cleveland*, para. 8. It is sometimes suggested that English law should adopt a general offence of 'child abuse' or 'child sexual abuse'; but it would seem difficult to define such an offence sufficiently clearly to satisfy the criterion that the law should be knowable in advance to those accused of violating it – a principle described as, 'of major importance in our criminal justice system' by the Law Commission, which also thought it 'right as a matter of constitutional principle' that the terms of the law should be 'clearly stated in a criminal code the terms of which have been deliberated upon by a democratically elected legislature': *A Criminal Code for England and Wales* (Law Commission, No. 177, 1989) para. 2.2.

14. See *R* v *Major* (1972) and *R* v Clarke (1975) as cited in D. A. Thomas, *Principles of Sentencing*, 2nd edn (London, Heinemann, 1979) p. 124; and most recently (on the appropriate sentencing policy in cases of incest) the judgement of the Court of Appeal in *Attorney General's Reference (no. 1 of 1989)* [1989] 1 W.L.R. 1117.

15. J. Gunn, G. Robertson, S. Dell and C. Way, *Psychiatric Aspects of Imprisonment* (London: Academic Press, 1978) p. 159.

16. Some attempts – notably the establishment of H. M. Prison Grendon

Underwood, and small units elsewhere – have been made to provide therapy for those offenders who would benefit: see J. Gunn *et al.*, *Psychiatric Aspects.*

17. See, for example, *A Child in Trust: The Report of the Panel of Enquiry into the Circumstances Surrounding the Death of Jasmine Beckford* (L. Blom-Cooper QC, Chairman) (1985).

18. See CIBA Foundation, *Child Sexual Abuse within the Family* (CIBA, 1984) p. 46; M. Chesterman, *Child Sexual Abuse and Social Work* (1985) p. 11. Far-reaching proposals for dealing with incest are made by J. Lloyd, 'The Management of Incest' (1982) JSWL 16.

19. See *R v Harrow London Borough, ex parte D* [1989] 3 W.L.R. 1293, CA, approving *R v Norfolk CC Social Services Department ex parte M* [1989] Q.B. 619.

20. Metropolitan Police and Bexley Social Services, Child Sexual Abuse, Joint Investigative Project (1987).

21. *Report of the Inquiry into Child Abuse in Cleveland*, para 6.79. The Inquiry was chaired by the Rt. Hon. Lord Justice Butler-Sloss, DBE.

22. See the helpful guidance given in 'Working Together, A Guide to Arrangements for Inter-agency Co-operation for the Protection of Children from Abuse' (London: DHSS and Welsh Office, 1988).

23. Part 3, para. 11.

24. Lloyd, 'The Management of Incest'. The question of the relationship between acceptance of culpability and treatment of the family unit, and the respective roles of the agencies is controversial; the present author would suggest that more research needs to be done on the (frequently repeated) assertion that victims of abuse often feel a need that the abuser be found to have offended against them. What kind of 'finding' would satisfy this need? For a helpful account of some of the issues in the context of practice at the Great Ormond Street Sexual Abuse Project in Children's Needs and Family Therapy, see A. Bentovim and B. Jacobs, 'The Case of Abuse', in E. Street and W. Dryden (eds) *Family Therapy in Britain* (London: Open University Press, 1988). See also Mark Chesterman, *Child Sexual Abuse and Social Work* (1985).

25. The fact that the rules supposedly protective of the innocent were manifestly ineffective in that case is not of itself a satisfactory answer to the general point.

26. Paragraph 10.18.

27. The Butler-Sloss Report sets out its understanding of the limited powers of a local authority at paras 16.2–14. The Report regarded the use of a Place of Safety Order in a situation in which there is no immediate danger to the child as 'wholly unjustified' (para. 16.14).

28. Per Dunn J., *re D* (*Justices' Decision: Review*) [1977] Fam. 158, 163.

29. Family Law Reform Act 1969, s. 7.

30. Law Commission Working Paper no. 101, para 3.32.

31. Ibid.

32. See paras 10.20–3, and 10.36.

33. Butler-Sloss Report, para. 10.36.

34. Hearsay evidence (e.g. that a child told a teacher that she had been

abused by a man) would be admissible in wardship proceedings: *re K (Infants)* [1965] AC 201. To the surprise of many, the Court of Appeal has now held that such evidence is not admissible in divorce-related custody proceedings in the County Court: *H* v. *H (Minor) (Child Evidence)* [1989] 3 W.L.R. 933. (*A Minor*); *re K (Minors)* (1989) *The Times*, 25 May, 1989. Moreover, it has been held that such evidence is not admissible in care proceedings: *Bradford Metropolitan City Council* v *K (Minors)* [1990] 2 W.L.R. 252. It is understood that provisions may be added to the Children Act 1989 to permit relevant evidence to be admitted.

35. *Re G (No. 2) (A Minor) (Child Abuse: Evidence)* [1988] 1 FLR 314. The judge in that case went on to say that there could be cases where 'although the court may be satisfied that no sexual abuse has taken place, the very fact that it has been alleged by a child against a parent suggests that, in the child's interests, some change in or control over the existing regime is required'; but it has subsequently been asserted [per Croom-Johnson IJ, *H* v. *H (Minor) (Child Abuse: Evidence)* [1989] 3 W.L.R. 933, 938, CA] that 'put baldly in that way' this statement cannot be right (apparently on the basis that the court can only act on evidence and must be satisfied on the balance of probabilities that the facts exist which justify its intervention.) However, it is suggested that if the admissible evidence does indicate that the child's welfare is at risk (for example, because the child suffers from a mental illness which leads him to make unfounded accusations) then the court would be entitled to intervene if necessary (for example, because the child's parents refused to recognise the need for treatment).

36. See the text the first Joseph Jackson Memorial Lecture given by the Lord Chancellor, Lord Mackay of Clashfern [1989] 139 *New LJ* 505.

37. Law Commission, no 172, para. 1.4.

Infertility treatment: a selective right to reproduce?

Julie Stone

Introduction

Infertility is a problem which affects many thousands of people in Britain each year. The incidence of infertility is said to be rising, with one recent survey suggesting that as many as one in six couples have difficulties in conceiving.[1] Yet despite the prevalence of infertility, sufferers frequently complain of the 'invisibility' of their problem, which until the introduction of *in vitro* fertilisation, and the ethical difficulties surrounding it, had been paid scant attention both by the medical profession and by society as a whole, and was regarded by the NHS as 'low priority'. Unlike IVF, GIFT, ZIFT and other new reproductive technologies, involving considerable technical expertise, the routine management of infertility is often a haphazard affair, with patients facing months or years of seemingly inconclusive tests and treatments.

Whilst IVF has undoubtedly been heralded by the media as a great success story, and few people have been unmoved by the pictures of smiling couples holding their artificially conceived child, this publicity has had the unfortunate effect of changing people's perceptions, so that many people think IVF is the main cure for infertility and is widely available to people who cannot conceive naturally. This, I believe, is unhelpful in a number of respects. First, the emphasis on 'hi-tech' solutions has diverted attention from the lack of funding and organising of infertility services at *all* levels. Secondly, it takes attention away from the causes of infertility and questioning what could be done to prevent infertility occurring. And thirdly, it raises the hopes and expectations of childless couples who may previously have accepted their childlessness but who are now prepared to subject themselves to endless investigative procedures in the hope that the new technologies will help them achieve a much sought after child. The excitement generated by the media has all but overlooked the incredibly low success rate of IVF at present, with less than 15% of IVF attempts resulting in live births.

Finally, by focusing on the success of a technique such as IVF, and by presisting with the portrayal of success only in terms of live births, the plight of those who will never conceive is made that much harder, and the equally important aim of encouraging people to come to accept their childlessness is virtually ignored.

In addition to these problems, the whole area of assisted reproduction raises some significant legal dilemmas. Is there a right to reproduce, which may be enforceable by law? Is there a right to infertility treatment and, if so, is this part of a general entitlement to health care? Is this a universal right, or one which is only available to certain people who fulfil certain criteria? In order to answer these questions we will have to have some regard to the nature of infertility, to see whether it fits in with existing 'illness' models, and to discover whether we think it is appropriate for such services to be provided on the NHS, or even at all.

I shall begin by posing the question 'is there a right to reproduce?' There is certainly a right not to have chidren in this country, manifested by the availability of free contraceptive services and access to legal terminations of pregnancy under the 1967 Abortion Act. The reverse question is rarely addressed. If such a right were to exist, what sort of claims would this create? Would it merely mean that people have the right not to be interfered with should they wish to reproduce or could it perhaps create a stronger right to be given certain assistance to bring about the desired outcome?

Additionally, given the facilities available for artificial reproduction, for whom should these services be available? Should there be any restrictions on acccess to IVF, with services provided on a first come first served basis, or should there be rigid selection criteria, as in the case of adoption? Has society a special duty of care towards artificially created children such that it should dictate who is best suited for parenting? Should we be governed, as in other areas of law, by the best interests of the child, or in this therapeutic setting, by the best interests of the patient? Furthermore, who should make this decision? Is it a question of clinical judgement or are wider social issues at stake? Finally, should there be any right of appeal against a refusal of acccess to an IVF programme and, if so, would the courts be an appropriate forum?

Reproduction—a rights issue?

What is meant by a 'right' to have children? Advocates of such a right point to the provisions of the European Convention for the Protection of Human Rights and Fundamental Freedoms which may be construed as implying such a right.[2] Article 8 speaks of 'the right to respect for his private and family life' and Article 12 states that 'men and women of marriageable age have the right to marry and to found a family'.

The question is whether this in any sense implies that there may be a positive right to have a child, or whether the Declaration merely implies that the individual should be protected from unwarranted interference with such 'rights'. It is easier to establish a right of non-interference than to create a corresponding duty on the part of others to provide positive assistance.

The common law has long recognised the principle that every person has the right to have his bodily integrity protected against invasion by others. Thus, in a medical context, failure to obtain a patient's consent to treatment may give rise to a claim of assault or negligence.[3] This would quite clearly preclude, for example, non-consensual sterilisation. The rights referred to in the European Convention of Human Rights could be interpreted as meaning that people may expect protection against state intervention with their reproductive capacities. These provisions would be protective rather than enabling, perhaps with a view to preventing eugenic programmes of the type found in the United States in the earlier part of this century. If this were the case, an action for damages would be available to anyone sterilised against his or her will.

But beyond this right of non-interference, is there something more fundamental in the nature of reproduction which merits special protection? Is there, in short, a fundamental right to reproduce?

In a number of reported decisions concerning sterilisation, courts have referred to such a right. What is the extent of this right? Is it a basic human right, an absolute right to be exercised by anyone who is capable of reproduction; or is it something less than an absolute right, to be exercised only by those whom society allows to exercise a free choice?

Support for the former view is found in a judgement of Heilbron

J. in *Re D*,[4] a case which concerned the proposed sterilisation of an 11-year-old girl suffering from Sotos syndrome. There it was said: 'The type of operation proposed is one which involves the deprivation of a basic human right, namely the right of a woman to reproduce.'[5] Heilbron J concluded that to perform a sterilisation on a woman for non-therapeutic reasons and without her consent would be a violation of that right. The learned judge's authority for so describing this right is uncertain, and on these facts of the case the decision not to sterilise was made in the best interests of the child.

LaForest J., in the Canadian case of *Re Eve*[6], whose views corresponded closely to those expressed by Heilbron J. in *Re D*, spoke of the 'grave intrusion on a person's rights' of sterilisation of a mentally incompetent person in these circumstances and referred to the 'fundamental right to bear children', declaring that sterilisation is unlawful in these circumstances unless carried out for therapeutic reasons. This argument was rejected by Lord Hailsham in *Re B*[7] who said that 'to talk of the basic right to reproduce of an individual who is not capable of knowing the causal connection between intercourse and childbirth, the nature of pregnancy, what is involved in delivery, unable to form maternal instincts or to care for a child appears to me wholly to part company with reality'.[8] He went on to say that Heilbron J. was correct in describing the right of a woman to reproduce as a basic human right and appreciated that there existed the so-called 'great privilege of giving birth', but in the present case the patient's handicaps 'render her incapable of ever exercising that right or enjoying that privilege'.[9]

On this rationale, it would seem that inherent in the notion of possessing a right to reproduce is the ability to appreciate that right and the ability to exercise a choice. The ramifications of such an argument, if extended to other areas of human rights, do not need to be spelt out.

Extending this argument, the right to reproduce, insofar as a right exists, is a right to choose to reproduce, which is better regarded as an aspect of the fundamental right to self-determination.[10] This in turn presupposes the ability to make an informed choice, and in the absence of such an ability a decision will be made on the patient's behalf based on the perceived best interests of the patient, as determined by the medical profession.

Moreover, it has been argued that the right to reproduce could, if applied rigidly, in these circumstances, conflict with other equally important 'rights' which we profess to value, such as the right to liberty. The evidence suggests that in the absence of sterilisation such patients would have to be continually supervised and have their freedom severely curtailed. In the Canadian case of *Re K*,[11] the judge, in deciding whether to authorise a hysterectomy, weighed the right to reproduce against the patient's right to be protected against the pain and suffering which would have resulted without the operation, and he concluded that the 'meaningless retention of the right to reproduce' would have directly conflicted with that equally important right.[12]

If the right to reproduce is no more than a right to choose, it will be even harder to derive from a Declaration of Human Rights a positive right of assistance to found a family.[13]

It is one thing to say one has a right not to be sterilised against one's will, but it is a very different thing to suggest that one must be provided with means to achieve reproduction. In this context, the right to found a family and to marry may be usefully contrasted. Uniacke points out that if the Declaration were to be cited in support of funding infertility services, a case would have to be made out that this right to reproduce is different from the recognised interpretation of the right to marry, which is essentially a positive right.[14] As she says:

> [The] exercise of the right to marry is something which is principally up to individuals themselves to organise. Corresponding obligations on the part of others, and the State, are strictly limited, even though being unmarried can be a source of distress, in some cases a life's ambition unfulfilled.

In legal terms, then, it is very difficult to establish an absolute right to have a child and virtually impossible to suggest that a right to found a family imposes a duty of positive assistance on the part of others. This has a bearing not only on access to infertility services, but also on the related areas of adoption and surrogacy.[15]

Alternative justifications

If a right of access to infertility services cannot be established by reference to a right to reproduce, some other basis of entitlement to these services must be found. One obvious solution is to describe infertility services as treatment, and say that access to infertility treatment is an integral part of access to health care. The problem with this approach is that it relies on a number of unresolved assumptions which cannot go unchallenged, viz can relieving infertility properly be described as treatment? Is infertility *per se* an illness which requires medical treatment? On the one hand, it may be argued that many people who are unable to have children lead perfectly 'normal', healthy lives. On the other hand, it may be argued that reproduction is a very basic desire or need, which unfulfilled can cause considerable distress. But if this is the case, is medical treatment the appropriate method of fulfilling an individual's desires? After all, we would all like different things at different times in our lives but rarely will medical intervention be the appropriate response. These questions are central to our understanding of the debate since the way in which we define and relate to infertility will have a material effect on the way in which we respond to it.

Assuming, for the sake of argument, that in some cases medical response is the appropriate way to deal with the problem of infertility, we must now ask ourselves, to whom should our existing infertility services be available? Should it be a 'first come first served' basis? Do married couples have the strongest claim to these services? Should we develop certain criteria, as in the case of adoption? Let us explore these options in detail. Since our society does not seek to prevent fertile people from reproducing naturally, whatever their status, sexual preference or income, why then, it may be asked, are these factors relevant in the context of assisting infertile people to reproduce artificially? Should society be controlling, directly and indirectly, in the context of 'artificial' reproduction, that which it cannot control in the ordinary course of events?

The widespread restriction on infertility treatments to 'stable' heterosexual couples, who are either married or in a long-standing relationship is a notable feature of clinics providing these services. If questioned about this policy, the usual response is to cite the best interests of the child, implying that if special responsibility is being taken to bring a child into the world artificially, a duty exists to ensure that the child will be born into a 'good' home.

I intend to show that value-laden decision-making of this sort is fraught with difficulties. Clearly, the question of what constitutes a good home depends entirely on the moral value system of the decision-maker. In the absence of empirical evidence that one type of environment is better than another, the decision will be entirely subjective. In addition to this, we must ask ourselves whether this is a decision properly taken by the doctor in charge of the programme, whose clinical judgement will ultimately determine who receives treatment. Are doctors uniquely competent to decide who will be fit parents? Indeed, apart from the question of *medical* suitability for a particular treatment, we should ask whether this is a medical decision at all or whether it is rather a moral, social and political question.

We must critically examine the basis on which services are currently provided and see whether there are alternative models for selection. In the majority of major reports on reproductive technologies, the importance of heterosexual relationships is taken for granted. IVF and artificial insemination are considered beneficial because they can give people a 'normal' family life, this commitment to normal family life being expressed in the United Nations Declaration of Human Rights, which states in Article 16, part 3: 'The family is the natural and fundamental group unit of society, and is entitled to protection by society and the State'.

Inherent in this heterosexual norm is the assumption that only married couples are considered best fit for parenthood. What we must ask ourselves is whether in a society such as ours, where 'broken homes' and single-parent units are increasingly prevalent, this should be the yardstick against which to measure acceptable parenthood. As Stanworth points out, the vision of the traditional family is sharply at odds with the experience of many men, women and children in Britain today, with the proportion of births conceived outside marriage steadily increasing. In addition to this, approximately 1 in 3 marriages end in divorce, with the result that the activity of raising children takes place less and less often in the context of a lasting marriage. This being the case, it is no longer wholly accurate to describe the conventional nuclear family as the norm and it is taking it one step further to suggest that anything other than such a family is necessarily an inappropriate unit for parenthood.[16]

Yet is precisely on the basis of that belief that infertility treatments are currently withheld from single women and lesbians, irrespective of the stability of the individuals and relationships in question. It would perhaps be different if studies had shown that the traditional model was optimum in terms of child rearing and that in addition, alternative models were necessarily harmful to the children of such units. Studies which suggest that children from broken homes living with one parent suffer emotionally must be looked at critically in the context of a deliberate choice to rear a child alone in a stable, loving environment. My point is that each application for IVF should be looked at critically on its merits rather than prejudged according to an individual consultant's preconceived views as to societal 'norms'. To discriminate against single women and lesbians in this area is as unacceptable as discriminating against them in the provision of health care generally.

Even the members of the Warnock Committee were aware that in determining criteria for suitability for IVF: 'No expression of their own personal feelings would be a credible basis for recommendation.'[17] Yet they went on to conclude:

> We believe that as a general rule, it is better for children to be born into a two-parent family, with both father and mother, although we recognise that it is impossible to predict with any certainty how lasting such a relationship will be.[18]

What then of the fact that decisions such as suitability for parenthood are routinely taken by the doctor? As I have tried to show, these questions raise political, social and moral issues. Whilst a doctor can judge which patients are likely to respond to various treatments, it is hardly a medical matter to decide who will make a good parent.

The issue can be seen even more clearly in the context of AID which represents the opposite end of the scale to 'hi-tech' procedure such as IVF and embryo transfer. The first question one might ask is why AID has been medicalised at all? The technical expertise required is minimal, and self-insemination can be just as successful in achieving a pregnancy.

The answer is linked to the medicalisation of reproduction generally, and highlights the fact that doctors effectively control who may or may not become pregnant. As Kennedy points out,[19] once an idea is seen as a matter for doctors, it is inevitable that doctors will establish criteria to satisfy before providing the service. The choice of criteria represents not medical factors, but the values and prejudices of the individual doctor.

Moreover, unlike other jurisdictions, which have now held the refusal to provide AID to single women as discriminatory,[20] the White Paper on Human Fertilisation and Embryology actually proposes that AID should become a criminal offence in the absence of an appropriate licence from the Statutory Licensing Authority.[21] Those who threaten the stability of the traditional family model may thus face prosecution in the future. The implications of decisions of this nature are far too important to be left in the hands of doctors. Whether a hospital ethics committee would be more suitable for these decisions is questionable. But such decisions, if they are to be taken at all, must be as a result of rational deliberation.

Might there be a better basis for treatment? One possibility would be to provide services according to medical need. If, as Warnock has said, a fundamental conclusion of the Warnock Committee was that infertility is a condition deserving a medical remedy, then infertility services should be equally available to all infertile people in need of treatment. Singer and Wells[22] suggest that need can be established by the strength of a desire for a child. Given that IVF is often seen as a last resort treatment and is withheld until all other avenues have been explored, (often including tubal surgery), it could be said that anyone who is prepared to experience the trauma of infertility investigations has evinced a sufficient desire to reproduce, forming a basis for entitlement. This desire is not unique to stable married couples and, as Singer and Wells point out, irrespective of people's sexual mores, the psychological pressures of IVF are so great that nobody undergoes such treatment without the highest motivation.

This approach is not without some difficulty. Since medical need, in the absence of a physiological complaint, is expressed by the desire to have a child, could it be argued that some infertile people are needier than others? Would, for example, a couple who have never been able to bear children have a greater right to treatment than a couple who already have one or more children but are having problems conceiving on a subsequent occasion? Should people who have, for example, been unable to conceive within 18 months be sent home for a further period? What of someone who has been voluntarily sterilised and whose personal circumstances have subsequently changed such that he/she is now seeking a reversal of that operation? Has that person 'used up' his/her share of limited health care resources? What is the position of the couple who have had one child by IVF and would like another? Must they return to the back of the queue? Ideally one would like to treat all of the above patients, but given the underfunding of the NHS and the low priority awarded to infertility services, this is unlikely to happen.

Although the Warnock Committee rejected the idea of laying

down hard and fast rules for selection,[23] it has been suggested that it would be desirable to draw up certain criteria to apply in these situations, rather like the selection criteria for adoption. These might include a provision to the effect that people should not be allowed IVF unless they can afford to provide for a child. Such sentiment has been expressed in Sweden, where it has been said that to have a child is not an absolute human right, and 'insemination should be allowed only on the condition that the child who is to be born is thereby offered a favourable upbringing.'[24] Once again we must question the idea of placing restrictions on the infertile which we do not place on the fertile.

The parallel of adoption criteria serves as a useful comparison. In selecting parents for adoption, the agencies are bound to consider the child's best interests first and foremost. Thus, previous experience of child rearing or other similar experience is considered an important element in determining suitability for adoption. This ironically works against couples with primary infertility who do not have children of their own. What then should the emphasis be in the case of providing infertility treatment? No doubt some regard must be given to any prospective child, and this would include taking precautionary measures such as checking whether candidates have a history of child abuse. Perhaps a medical history would be appropriate and an upper age limit placed upon women wishing to embark upon infertility treatment.

However, unlike criteria for adoption, the therapeutic nature of the doctor–patient relationship demands that the emphasis in this context be firmly related to the needs of the patient. The enterprise of relieving infertility is different in nature to adoption, and it is because of these conflicting aims that adoption is not a satisfactory answer for the childless (coupled with the very small number of healthy babies to adopt), which must be remembered when discussing non-medical solutions to infertility.

It has been suggested that IVF could be provided as a form of compensation for wrongful sterilisation, but this presents obvious difficulties. Whilst this has a certain retributive appeal, it would be extremely hard to accommodate it within an existing legal framework. The obvious difficulty is that a doctor, in performing IVF, can only be expected to act in accordance with the professional standard. He or she cannot guarantee a pregnancy or a live birth. A form of damages which consisted of unlimited access to medical treatment with no promise of an ultimate remedy would not be workable in practice.

Another basis of justification for infertility treatment is that infertility is an illness, and thus treatment to overcome infertility and have a child is an appropriate response. This argument is not without difficulty. Infertile people are not ill as such, and infertility need not be a bar to a perfectly healthy existence. It is only when the diagnosis of infertility is coupled with a strong desire to have children that couples may become profoundly distressed and even obsessional in their attempts to fulfil that desire.

Infertility in one sense is better described as a symptom rather than a disease. It may be that techniques such as IVF do nothing to alter the existing condition, but respond to the major symptom by using technology to provide a child. Is this an inappropriate basis for treatment? Robert Edwards, co-pioneer of IVF in this country, argues that most medical treatment is similarly symptomatic in nature. He cites insulin, false teeth and glasses as examples of medical treatment that do not correct the patient's condition but modify its expression.[25]

There is still uneasiness about treating people's desires (in this case the sometimes profound desire for a child) and infertility treatment has been compared to cosmetic surgery as a questionable recipient of NHS funding. In my opinion, infertility is sufficiently similar to other conditions which are treated on the NHS, albeit by providing symptomatic relief, that a right to infertility treatment should be an integral part of a right to health care.

Others take the view, however, that the status of infertility as an illness is so dubious that treatment should be provided only if people are prepared to pay for it themselves. Such is the position in America where health insurance does not cover infertility treatment. Unfortunately, a similar situation is emerging here and we must ask ourselves whether we want a situation where the wealthy infertile are able to reproduce whilst their less affluent counterparts are not. Only one clinic in Britain is funded entirely by the NHS, the result being that most IVF in the UK is carried out in private clinics in return for fees. A current estimate for IVF is £2000–£2500 per treatment, and two or three treatments are not uncommon.

Clearly, assisted reproduction is not accessible to everyone in need. The lack of NHS funding of infertility discriminates against those who cannot afford private treatment and this, coupled with the 'suitability' test, renders the 'right to reproduce' a rather meaningless concept.

IVF and the Courts

Before leaving the question of selection, I would like to consider the options open to someone who has been refused access to an IVF programme. The Warnock Committee acknowledged that on certain occasions, individual practitioners would decline to treat a particular patient, and their recommendation was as follows: 'in cases where consultants decline to provide treatment they should always give the patient a full explanation of the reason'.[26] A stated aim of this recommendation was to enable patients to exercise a right to seek a second opinion. However, given the time it takes to see a consultant for the first time, waiting for an appointment with a second consultant is likely to be a similarly protracted affair. Moreover, where one consultant has deemed a person 'unsuitable', there is every chance that a second opinion will have the same outcome.

Should there be, as a last resort, the possibility of reviewing such a decision via the courts? Is this an appropriate matter for judicial review, and is it an area that should be judicialised? The issue is discussed in the High Court decision of *R.* v. *Ethical Committee of St Mary's Hospital (Manchester) ex parte Harriott.*[27]

In that case, the applicant, who was unable to have children naturally, was placed on the waiting list of the hospital's *in vitro* fertilisation unit. Her name was subsequently removed when it was discovered that she had previously been rejected by the local social services authority as a prospective adoptive parent, because of a former criminal record for offences relating to prostitution. She sought judicial review: first, of the hospital ethical committee's refusal to give its own recommendation to the IVF unit, and secondly, of the consultant's decision to remove her name from the waiting list. Although she succeeded in obtaining leave to apply for judicial review, her application was refused by Schiemann J.

The case raises several important questions. First, should the decision of the hospital ethics committee be subject to judicial review? It is crucial to establish whether this is procedurally appropriate, otherwise future cases will fall at the first hurdle. Judicial review in broad terms lies only against a decision of a public authority or agency vested with public law functions. In the *Harriott* case, the ethical committee had no source of power in law

– there had been no statutory duty to set up the committee and there was no statutory duty on the committee either to decide or advise. Rather, it was said, the committee was essentially an informal body with the function of providing a forum for discussion among professionals. Arguably though, an ethical committee could be regarded as forming an integral part of the National Health Service structure; this structure, in principle, being amenable to judicial review. Even if the ethical committee is not itself an appropriate respondent for an application for judicial review, then the NHS, as provider of the service might be. Decisions as to whether to give or withhold treatment, are governed by public law. The NHS has a statutory duty to provide services for the treatment of illness, which is delegated by the Secretary of State through the health authorities to individual units. In *Harriott*, Schiemann J. assumed that the individual consultant's decisions are amenable to judicial review.

However, and anomalously, it is unlikely that judicial review would be appropriate in the private sector, as there the decision to treat is founded on contract. It may, none the less, be an implied term of the contract that a person will not be turned away unfairly or irrationally.

Was the ethical committee in breach of its duties failing to give advice to the consultant? Schiemann J. decided that the committee was not under a duty to provide independent advice to the IVF unit and had the power to advise the consultant to make the decision herself. As to the question of abuse of discretion, Schiemann J. said that where advice is given, it may on occasion be possible to review that advice, stating obiter that, if the committee had advised that IVF should not be offered to 'anyone who was a Jew or coloured', the courts might well grant a declaration that such policy was illegal. This, however, would be based on clear legislation prohibiting racial discrimination in the provision of services.[28] Must there be such legislation, or could judicial control of discretion be exercised whenever discretion was exercised improperly, for example, by taking account of irrelevant considerations? If this were the case, then judicial review may be relevant where infertility treatment is refused on the basis, for example, of age of the father or sexual orientation of partners requesting treatment. This though would leave the judiciary, rather than the medical profession, with the important task of deciding whether, for example, homosexuality is a relevant factor in determining suitability for parenthood.

The duty to act fairly is one which affects the Health Service structure as a whole and may affect an individual consultant's decision. In *Harriott*, the applicant contended that her consultant's decision to remove her from the waiting list was a violation of the duty to act fairly, amounting to procedural impropriety. Although Schiemann J. decided that, on the facts, the consultant had not acted unfairly, he did not say expressly whether such a duty exists. Freedom from discrimination is an underlying feature of English administrative law. Discrimination should apply not only to race, sex and marital status, but equally to stereotyping and prejudice. Where decisions of refusal to treat are taken, they must be reached through a fair procedure. It is fundamental that this is borne in mind when making these 'medical' decisions.

It is unacceptable that matters of such grave importance be tackled in this fashion. Bringing questions concerning micro-allocation of resources before the courts does nothing to promote fair health care administration in the long run, and fails to confront the central issue, which is the current low priority attached to funding the treatment of problems of infertility in this country.

I have tried to show that the concept of a 'right to reproduce' is, at best, a right not to have one's reproduction interfered with, and even that right is less secure since the House of Lords judgement in *F* v *West Berkshire Health Authority*. Attempts to secure better funding for the treatment of infertility will thus have to seek an alternative justification, since our apparent commitment to the nuclear family does not seem to extend to those requiring positive assistance to reproduce, and excludes, by its very definition, access to those who do not fit the traditional model.

Notes and references

1. This survey studied a group of 708 couples living within a single health district in England. The results showed that at least one in six couples needed specialist help at some time in their lives, 71 per cent of whom were trying for their first baby.
2. Four articles of the European Convention may be of relevance: Article 2 protects by law 'everyone's right to life'. Article 3 says 'no one shall be subjected to torture or to inhuman or degrading treatment or punishment'. Article 8 speaks of the 'right to respect for his private and family life'. Article 12 says 'Men and women of marriageable age have the right to marry and found a family'.
3. See, for example, *Sidaway* v. *Governors of the Bethlem Royal Hospital* [1985] AC 871.

4. *Re D* (A Minor) (Wardship: Sterilisation) (1976) Fam. 185 (1976) 1 All ER 326.
5. Ibid. 332.
6. *Re Eve* (1986) 2 S.C.R. 388.
7. *Re B* (A Minor) (Wardship: Sterilisation) (1987) 2 All ER 206.
8. Ibid. 213d.
9. (1987) 2 All ER at 214e.
10. The right to control one's body was accepted by the House of Lords in *Sidaway* v. *Governors of Bethlem Royal Hospital* (1985) 1 All ER 643. In that case, Lord Scarman said that the right of self-determination may be seen as a 'basic human right protected by the common law'.
11. *Re K* (1985) 4 WWR 724.
12. Ibid. 756.
13. Pioneers of IVF have none the less relied on the provisions of such declaration to justify their work, see, for example, Carl Wood and Ann Westmore in *Test-Tube Conception* (London: Allen and Unwin, 1983) p. 102.
14. Suzanne Uniacke, *In Vitro* Fertilisation and the Right to Reproduce', *Bioethics*, vol. 1 (1987) no. 3.
15. So, for example, a couple who apply to adopt a child are in no sense guaranteed to be selected as parents. Similarly, where surrogacy would be a possible way of bypassing female infertility, there is equally no absolute right to have a child in that there can be no absolute duty on another woman to provide her services as a surrogate.
16. Indeed, it is already accepted that in certain circumstances a single person may adopt a child by virtue of s. 11 of the Children Act 1975.
17. Preface to the Warnock Report on Human Fertilisation and Embryology in Warnock, *'A Question of Life'* (1985).
18. Warnock Report, para. 2.11.
19. This point is raised by Kennedy in reference to AID, in his article 'What's a Medical Decision', reprinted in I. Kennedy, *'Treat Me Right'* (Oxford: Clarendon Press, 1988) pp. 19–31.
20. See, for example, the Canadian province of Saskatchewan, where refusal to inseminate a single woman is taken as a discriminatory measure.
21. Paragraph 27 of the White Paper states. 'It will be forbidden to use gametes donated by a third party to create, by artificial means, an embryo inside the body without an appropriate licence from the S.L.A.'
22. P. Singer and D. Wells, *The Reproduction Revolution* (New York: Oxford University Press, 1984) p. 69.
23. Warnock Report, para. 2.13.
24. See Delaisi De Parseval and Fagot-Largeault in *Bioethics* vol. 2 (1988) no. 2.
25. See Robert Edwards, 'Fertilisation of Human Eggs *in vitro*: Morals, Ethics and the Law', *Quarterly Review of Biology*, vol. 49 (1974) pp. 13–14.
26. Warnock Report, para. 2.13.
27. *The Times*, 27 October 1987.
28. Race Relations Act 1976, s. 7.

Making public policy on medical–moral issues

Ian Kennedy and Julie Stone

Part I

A review of this kind should not concern itself with a detailed exegesis of recent cases and statutes touching on medical law. Now that there is a growing number of commentators on medical law, such detailed work can safely be left to others.[1] What we can do instead is to stand back and survey the general scene.

From this wider perspective, perhaps the single most interesting theme is a recurring one: the making of public policy in areas of medical–moral concern. We have in mind the following analytical process. First, as regards any particular issue, is there a need for there to be some public policy? The matter could otherwise be left to be resolved in whatever way groups or individuals think best. Secondly, if there is a need for some public policy (and the criteria relevant to determine this question are both important and elusive), how is it to be made? This is often the same question as who is to make it. Thirdly, what form should the public policy take, if indeed there is to be any? Should it take the form of a policy statement such as a government circular, a set of guidelines or a code of practice, or should it take the form of law, i.e. statute?

When set out in this way, this seems an obvious enough set of enquiries. Also it would seem to recommend itself as the process policy makers should go through before arriving at any particular position on any matter. It will come as no surprise, therefore, that nothing like it happens in real life.

The present approach

The manner in which we decide whether to make public policy on any medical–moral issue and what form such policy should take could (politely) be described as haphazard. If issues attract the attention of the press, utterances are delivered from those whom the press judge capable of having a view, and then silence, until the next crisis/climax/breakthrough. The noise made by the press or interested parties may, however, on other occasions persuade Her Majesty's Government to set up some *ad hoc* group or committee to examine a particular issue. A report will emerge. It may, or may not, address the questions we have posed concerning the making of public policy. It may or may not, in any event, be acted upon. The group or committee will then fade into the night, never to meet again. Very occasionally, quite unpredictably, Her Majesty's Government surprises everyone and decides not just that some public policy statement is needed but that it should take the form of law. A Bill is drafted and, often, muddled through.

Most commonly these days, however, all the nice analytical questions about public policy are simply ignored. Some frustrated person (or group), unable to find guidance elsewhere or faced with a *de facto*, but unstated, public policy which is at least contentious, will approach the courts. The difficult questions about whether we need any public policy and the role of law are swept aside. The law is invoked and must respond. Public policy is made. The courts will determine it, regardless of their suitability for the task. Furthermore, the public policy will take the form of law.

Examples   Examples of this process (if it can be so described) of making public policy on medical–moral issues largely by default, if at all, are not hard to find. We will examine them in greater detail later, but refer briefly to them here. Rumblings, for example, about mapping the genome or the adequacy of the supply of organs for transplants surface in the press from time to time and then drop out of public attention. Committees such as those chaired by Baroness Warnock[2] or Dr John Polkinghorne[3] were set up when the pressure exerted from various quarters was strong but when there was no clear strategy for government to adopt which would meet its eternal (and sole) preoccupation, short-term electoral popularity. It is a truism worth repeating that committees allow government to remain inactive while appearing to have acted. As it happens, both of the committees we refer to did address the issues of public policy making. They agreed on the need for a stated public policy but did not agree on the form which that policy should take. Warnock opted largely for legislation, particularly the use of the criminal law. Polkinghorne preferred non-statutory guidelines.

Legislation can be seen in the Surrogacy Arrangements Act 1985, an immediate (and some may think too hasty) response to Warnock, which was immediately followed by attempts to amend it (which failed) through the Surrogacy Arrangements (Amendment) Bill 1985, (that Parliament found time for two such bills when lack of parliamentary time is given by government as a reason for inaction in so many other areas is evidence either of a certain lack of candour or of, at best, an odd system of priorities operated by government). The swift appearance and passage of the Human Organ Transplants Act in 1989 is further evidence of a tendency to respond to the sensational. Furthermore, it is a matter almost of amazement to some that this Act should breeze through while the very many efforts to reform the Human Tissue Act 1961, so as to confront the real problem of transplantation, i.e. the chronic shortage of organs, have all failed.

Examples or problems being taken to the courts for them to resolve *faute de mieux* are now becoming only too common. A dozen years ago medical law cases were almost as rare as hens' teeth. Now they are commonplace. They may still be characterised as cases on negligence, malpractice, family law, criminal law, or vicarious and primary liability rather than medical law. In fact, however, they raise central issues of public policy: how best should the disequilibrium of power between professional and client, doctor and patient, be managed, a disequilibrium demonstrated by the answers usually given to questions such as: Who is a fit parent? When, if ever, is it justified to sterilise someone who cannot consent? Who should determine how resources should be allocated within the Health Service? That public policy, if needed, cannot always be best made by an institution as busy and ill-equipped for appropriate analysis and reflection as a court, pressed to decide a case between adversaries, must be obvious. But the one thing a court cannot do is refuse to decide a case once it has taken jurisdiction. So, by default, public policy is made and it is made in the form of law.

Additional drawbacks of the present approach

Accountability   The inadequacy of the current state of affairs when it comes to making public policy must be clear to all. But the problem does not stop there. Proceeding in the way we do creates further problems or hidden costs which must not be ignored. The first is the issue of accountability: the accountability of the medical professional and research scientist. There can be little doubt that an effective and institutionalised system of ensuring the accountability of the medical professional (just as with any other professional group) is both necessary and desirable. It reflects the spirit of the times and seeks to provide a proper means of distributing power between professional and client. As such it is a significant public policy issue.

But, if the response to medical–moral concerns is to appoint an *ad hoc* committee which produces *ad hoc* guidelines, or is to leave matters to the medical profession or scientific researchers, or pass the odd (in every sense) bit of legislation, any coherent system of accountability is doomed. The central questions of accountability (to whom? as regards what? and how?) receive different answers in different contexts (if they are answered at all). As regards the courts, in case it be thought that they have become the central mechanism for accountability, it is as well to remember that litigation plays a very small role in the accountability of doctors and even less of research scientists. Furthermore, the courts, finding themselves a mechanism of accountability whether they like it or not, have over the last decade systematically declined to develop any principles of accountability beyond professional self-regulation. Thus, by default or perhaps by intention, we see by the end of the 1980s a bewildering number of systems of accountability, all different, all hard to operate by the public (for whom they are supposed to exist) and all, therefore, serving to preserve the entrenched power of the medical profession while appearing to share power at every turn.

Lobbying   There is a second hidden cost of the absence of any systematic method of determining the shape and form of public policy which is itself of considerable concern as a matter of public policy. Into the vacuum of analysis and reflection step the single-interest lobbies and the powerful figures of the great and the good.

The result may be a one-sided appraisal of a particular issue. The current consideration of the rights and wrongs of research on embryos echoes with claims (arguably based on no good scientific argument) that 'breakthroughs' in the prevention of genetic disability depend critically on such research, such that opponents of research can be castigated as cruel and uncaring. Generally, stress may be laid, for example, on possible 'breakthroughs' or cures and not on possible costs, whether in terms of diverted resources or patients' rights. Or, there may be a strident polarisation of views with powerful lobbies exchanging epithets in mutual incomprehension, such that evidence and analysis become the first casualties. Neither of these nor even their less extreme variants can be the right way to regulate our affairs. Yet they thrive in the absence of anything better.

A national commission

Against this background, it is no surprise that calls are periodically made for some kind of institution which will allow the proper shaping and formation of public policy in areas of medical–moral concern. One of us called for a national commisison some seven years ago.[4] Baroness Warnock attracted considerable attention when she echoed this call in 1988.[5] And many others have made the same point: that there is a need for a single body able to reflect on issues of concern and assist in the formulation of public policy in a coherent and consistent manner.

Of course, the idea has its opponents. Some see such a body as a threat to their current power and they are right to do so. But, if you believe that public policy should not be determined solely by powerful groups then their opposition can be discounted. Others object that the scale of the exercise is too great, the field too extensive, the pace of development too fast for any single body to come up with anything worthwhile. The rebuttal is simple. The work of the President's Commission in the US (which effectively extended over three to four years) gives the lie to this objection.[6] Sixteen volumes of work across the range of medical–moral concerns, which together represent the very best in scholarship and practical policy making, appeared in that short time. Since then, countries such as France, Belgium, Denmark, Netherlands, West Germany,[7] Australia[8] and the USA[9] (in a new form) have all established national commissions. They cannot all be wrong. If those who advise government choose none the less to ignore this evidence, there must be reasons for their opposition. What these are can only be guessed at. They must be strong to cause government to ignore a case which so many believe has been made out for years. As Sir John Junor would have it, 'We should be told'.

Recent developments

Case law   It is not surprising, in the light of what we have said, that the story of recent developments in public policy making is disappointing. Developments in medical law, as part of that story, are equally disappointing. Issues have continued to land in the lap of the courts willy nilly. The courts have dealt with them, perhaps, with the notable exception of *Re F* (1989)[10] with a continuing lofty disinterest in developing a body of coherent principles governing the practice of medicine and the doctor–patient relationship. Medical law is still regarded as no more than an applied area of torts or family law. The consequence is a continued failure to recognise and take account of the underlying principles of medical ethics which should inform the creation of any particular legal rule and ensure the coherent development of medical law as a whole.

Legislation   As we have seen, Parliament has demonstrated its characteristic reluctance to become involved, save when in an extraordinary surge of activity it was moved to pass the Human Organ Transplants Act 1989. The spectacle of public policy being made on the hoof was less than impressive. That the public policy embraced so vigorously by Parliament in proposing this legislation was completely at odds with the political philosophy of the present government went largely unremarked. We do not suggest that the view reflected in the Act, that the sale of organs for transplant should not be permitted, is wrong. What we suggest is that the abandonment of support for enterprise and the market place in favour of an aggressive paternalism, backed by criminal sanctions, warranted rather more political reflection than it received. So too did the ready conclusion that the sale of organs was inevitably morally wrong. The arguments are not easy.[11] They certainly do not all point in one direction. But, most serious of all, there was no real reflection on why law was needed as the expression of public policy. There are complicated arguments here, often not understood by the non-lawyer. If rehearsed, the passage of the Act may be more carefully analysed. In essence, the argument is that, yes indeed, as with most issues, there are respectable moral arguments both for condemning and allowing the sale of organs. In many cases this would suggest the conclusion that people should be left to choose which position they prefer. In some cases, however, the choice should not properly be left to the individual. The state through its law should rightfully choose. Further, to ensure that its choice is respected and to signal the importance of the issue, the choice should be expressed in the form of law, the most serious of the forms of public policy making open to it.

All this has been said before. It is the very heart of the public policy debate: what is it about a moral issue which suggests that some form of public policy position is called for and what is it that warrants recourse to law? Regrettably it is rare for such questions to be raised and answered critically. Certainly it was not the case as regards the Human Organ Transplants Act.

The saga of the Warnock Report provides a further illustration of muddled or non-existent public policy analysis. First, Warnock recommended policy in the form of criminal law in a number of areas without offering reasons for this conclusion. Parliament (i.e. the government) differed, preferring no policy to one which might be divisive. An interested party stepped in, the Medical Research Council, and made policy, reflecting the majority view of Warnock, in the form of voluntary guidelines.[12] The government having run out of ways of avoiding action, finally produced a Bill[13] which on perhaps the single most important issue of principle, research on embryos, in effect simply says 'take your pick'.[14] This resort to the free vote may be entirely justifiable, but it is not entirely clear why it is avowedly the job of government to set policy in, for example, the case of the sale of organs, or the proposed restructuring of the National Health Service (with its morally contentious re-shaping of the doctor–patient relationship), but not in the case of research on embryos. The reason cannot be that embryo research is not a matter of party politics whereas the National Health Service is. This would not explain the government's decision to enact the Human Organ Transplants Act, since there is no party political issue at stake there. Thus, recourse to the 'free vote' as a form of public policy response is itself a complex and under-analysed phenomenon.

Guidelines Apart from action by way of legislation, the government has, as we have seen, also tinkered with medical–moral issues through the development of guidelines regarding, for example, fetal tissue transplants[15] and research ethics committees.[16] Both of these illustrate perfectly the *ad hoc* approach whereby people are brought together, expertise is developed, a particular issue is dealt with and the expertise is cast to the four winds. Then another group is formed, expertise acquired, the issue is dealt with and again the group disbands. The inefficiency is obvious. Equally obvious is the danger that common threads will be missed and a coherent policy recognising the interconnectedness of issues will go undeveloped.

Inaction While public policy making concerning those issues of medical–moral concern which attracted attention faltered and stuttered, other issues of the greatest medical–moral concern continued to be ignored or left to 'experts'. Two examples suffice. Genetic therapy and associated counselling, though raising the most complex of moral questions and touching the very nature of the society we create, proceed virtually untouched by any public policy pronouncement. If you will, we have no public policy on the matter. The other example involves the care of the patient who is not dying but is in what is known as a persistent vegetative state. This poses the most complex and agonising difficulties. Should the doctor or nurse, for example, continue to administer food and hydration or may they (or one) be withdrawn. Silence, in the form of any public policy, greets the question.

Part II

The argument so far has been concerned to demonstrate two points. The first is that the making of public policy and particularly its expression in the form of law is of critical importance in the field of medical–moral concerns yet goes unanalysed. The second is that we have at present no coherent system which would allow such analysis and deliberation. Legislation, self-regulation, exhortation, judicial decisions or silence coexist, with no obvious indicator of which may be resorted to in any particular case. That said, it is the courts which are taking the strain. Let us, therefore, analyse their performance in greater detail.

Role of the courts

As we have seen, the only circumstances in which public policy necessarily will be made, and made in the form of law, is when an issue is taken before the courts. That this is occurring more and more frequently indicates, in our view, both an obvious uncertainty as to what is permissible (what are the tolerated boundaries of medical practice and research?) and a desire to have some body, some institutional mechanism, to look to for guidance. How have the courts performed? The answer must be that they are at last beginning to improve. At least one reason why we take this view is that medical law is still very much in its infancy in terms of there being a body of developed doctrine. A heaven-sent opportunity exists for the courts, particularly the House of Lords, to provide thoughtful guidance for the future, indeed it could be said that it is their duty to do so. In the past the courts have not seemed anxious to seize this opportunity. This has made the reference by the courts to the threat of American-style litigation particularly odd. In their decisions, they have consistently avoided offering guidance on the law beyond that required by the immediate facts. No situation is more calculated to provoke American-style litigation. Obscurity breeds contention. It would appear that the courts are, however, slowly but reluctantly recognising this, as we shall suggest.

There is a justification for the courts' reluctance which may be offered. It is that they are, like it or not, stuck with a particular dispute between particular parties involving particular facts. In such circumstances, the court cannot be expected to reflect on the wider implications of its decision. It is not a legislature, dealing with the general. It is at best the interstitial legislator, filling in the odd gap, while leaving policy to Parliament. Indeed, Lord Scarman in the case of *McLoughlin* v *O'Brian*[17] elevated the distinction between principle (for the courts) and policy (for the legislature) virtually to the state of a constitutional theory. That the distinction, if it exists, is a distinction without a difference seems not to have troubled him. How, after all, can principle be applied save by making some judgement which in turn will reflect some policy position (unless you believe in some algebraic or logical theory of decision-making)?

There are several available rebuttals of this view which are particularly germane when it is recalled that we are dealing with issues which are largely matters of first impression – recognised to be of great importance but on which the law is so far silent. The first is that while the argument may be true of a court of first instance, it should not be true of the House of Lords, and many of the current medical law cases are decisions of the House of Lords. Secondly, the court, especially the House of Lords, *is* prepared, when it chooses, to expand on the law in general terms, devising whole schemes of law of general application. *Gillick*,[18] *Sidaway*[19] (where the House of Lords could simply have decided that on the facts Mrs Sidaway had failed to show she was not warned of the risks of the operation) and *Re F* (1989)[20] are cases which some at least of their Lordships were prepared to set aside the 'I am only a pragmatic judge' tendency. The alternative tendency, however, is still all too familiar, whereby the courts seem to adopt the entirely disingenuous proposition of Lord Donaldson MR that the common law is only 'common sense under a wig'.[21] The guidance this gives as to the state of the law is perhaps only slightly less obscure than Lord Donaldson's proposition in *Sidaway* that doctors must behave 'rightly'.[22] Of course, what is infuriatingly elusive for the analyst is determining when the court will be expansive and when it will be pragmatic. That it can be either is unquestionable.

Recent case law

With these points in mind, let us look at some of the more significant recent cases on medical law with an eye to the contribution they make to the formulation of coherent public policy in matters of medical–moral concern.

Re F (1989)[23]   In *Re F*, the House of Lords had to wrestle with the circumstances, if any, under which an adult incompetent female could be sterilised without her consent. Fundamentally, there were two issues for the court, the question of consent and the question of sterilisation. In its previous decision, *Re B* (1987)[24], the House of Lords had only to deal with the latter issue, since the female involved was a minor. This meant that if sterilisation was a permissable option, the court in the exercise of wardship jurisdiction could give consent to the operation on the girl's behalf. The way in which the House of Lords in *Re B* dealt with the sterilisation question disappointed many, to say the least. A distinct impression of unseemly haste attended the proceedings. She was four months short of her eighteenth birthday at the time of the hearing in the House of Lords (i.e. was soon to be beyond the reach of wardship jurisdiction which extends only to minors). An issue as charged as compulsory (or non-consensual) sterilisation received one day's hearing before the court at which certain fundamental issues, especially concerning the relevance and effect of the European Convention on

Human Rights received less than full attention. The decision of the House of Lords, that the decision whether or not to sterilise a young girl depended in law on whether it was 'in her best interests' to do so, seemed to many to demonstrate a lamentable reluctance on the part of the court to offer any real public policy guidelines. It is a commonplace that the term 'best interests' is a conclusion of social policy. It could not be further from the considered set of carefully analysed criteria that those caring for and about the mentally handicapped looked for. Yet the court refused to be drawn, falling back on the language of family law and thereby failing to recognise that this was a medical law case calling for a different analytical approach. The 'best interests' or welfare language of family law atomises the law, suggesting that each case is to be dealt with on its own facts and merits. Such an approach, reflecting as it does the recourse in medical ethics to situation ethics, is, of course, intellectually suspect since value solutions do not emerge from facts but from the values which are brought to those facts. But, more critically, it prevents the development of any articulated criteria concerning the propriety of sterilisation. And by so doing it runs the real risk of making any decision about sterilisation appear to be a matter of fact, of 'expert' opinion, which it decidedly is not. The views of 'experts' are relevant but only if they are given in response to questions which reflect a prior ethical analysis. By relying on the incantation of 'best interests' and offering nothing further by way of reasoned guidance, it could be said that the House of Lords failed in its duty to make sound public policy. Critically, echoing what we have said earlier, the House of Lords by resorting to the *ad hoc* approach of family law, failed to provide an adequate mechanism whereby those caring for a mentally handicapped girl may be held to account for their decision. If all is a matter of 'best interests' and if, as it would be said, experts may legitimately differ, any safeguards against the inappropriate use of sterilisation disappear. And, whatever was right in *Re B* (and we take no view on it), sterilisation must be inappropriate in some cases.

In the later case of *Re F* (1989), the House of Lords did significantly better in offering public policy guidelines. First, on the issue of consent the court, in a careful mix of legal scholarship and down-to-earth understanding, finally gave clear guidance on the lawfulness of treating an incompetent adult without consent. Proof of the fact that medical law is in its infancy is the fact that it was

1989 before this issue was finally resolved. A few purist die-hards continued to argue that it was trespass to touch an adult patient without consent, except in an emergency or in the circumstances contemplated by the Mental Health Act 1983. Most, however, assumed that the law simply did not require a mentally handicapped person with, for example, toothache to languish in pain. The justification for treating the patient could be found, they said, in those trusty standbys 'necessity'[25] or 'public interest'.[26] And this is what the House of Lords decided. No one, it was decided has the authority to consent to the treatment of an adult. Not even a court could do so, since the power to act as *parens patriae* was no longer vested in the court. This does not mean, however, the court went on, that an incompetent adult must go without needed treatment. If the treatment is indeed justified as being in the patient's best interests, then as a matter of public policy it is lawful to give it. Consent or its lack is, in this context, irrelevant. The use of 'best interests' can be justified here since it is a general principle intended as a starting-point for analysis, i.e. it is then open to others to argue that what may *prima facie* be in a patient's best interests may not be because of the type of treatment proposed in the particular circumstances of the patient.

So much for the consent issue; a classic example, if you will, of the court's realising the need for there to be public policy guidelines which, given the importance of the issue should take the form of law, and of the court's responding to this need.

What of the sterilisation issue? A first reading of the House of Lords' decision does not inspire confidence. The judges seem often to disagree, and where there is agreement it seems to be reminiscent of the 'best interests' approach adopted in *Re B* with a further and most regrettable twist. For the House of Lords seems to be saying that the test of whether a particular decision to sterilise is in the best interests of the woman is to be judged by reference to the case of *Bolam*.[27] Now *Bolam* is the case that decided the standard of care which a doctor must meet so as to comply with the duty of care owed to a patient; 'a doctor is not guilty of negligence if he acts in accordance with a practice accepted as proper by a responsible body of medical men skilled in that particular art'.[28] The standard of care required is that of a reasonably competent doctor. What does *Bolam* have to do with sterilisation cases? They are about such matters as the limits of what may permissibly be done to someone, the extent and meaning of human rights such as privacy, and the propriety of the use of medical solutions to deal with healthy people. The reference to *Bolam* would make it appear that a sterilisation operation may lawfully be carried out if the attending doctor, acting as a reasonable doctor, decides that it is in the best interests of the woman. By adopting such a view, the House of Lords would appear to be adopting a particularly narrow view of what public policy may demand. They would simply be handing the matter over to the 'experts'. Moreover they would be doing so in circumstances in which they did not retain any power of scrutiny, since any particular operation would be lawful if doctors said it was. The opportunity to put in place an institutionalised system of accountability would again have been ignored.

This is one reading of the House of Lords' decision. It is not, however, accurate. On closer examination, the House of Lords was clearly anxious to be seen to lay down public policy guidelines in this fraught area. And, just as significantly, they were anxious to explore the role which law could and should play in such guidelines.

The following points emerge from the case as important for our purposes. First, as we have seen, the House of Lords decided that it had no power to give or withhold consent to the non-consensual sterilisation of an adult, since no one in law has such authority. The House of Lords could, of course, have followed Lord Griffiths' advice and simply assumed this power,[29] but this was too great a step for the rest. None the less, they made it clear that they would expect a court to be consulted in every case of proposed sterilisation in such circumstances. It is hard to imagine any local authority or health authority ignoring this advice, if only to avoid explaining why they had not sought the advice of a court if anything subsequently went wrong. Thus, the first plank in building public policy guidelines is in place. The court signalled the importance of the issue. So important is it that it should never be done without the involvement of a court, even though the court technically has no power in the matter.

The House of Lords then went on to indicate, albeit without the clarity that could have been hoped for, the factors which a court should bear in mind in advising on the matter. As we have said, *prima facie* the House of Lords appeared to say that all that it will inquire into is what *Bolam* calls for: namely, whether the doctor has acted as a reasonably competent doctor. But there is more to it. Their Lordships, each in his own way, then set out the factors which a reasonable doctor (and, it is made clear, others in the care team) must take account of so as to be judged by the courts to have acted reasonably. Ordinarily, this would be a matter of expert evidence for doctors. This is, after all, what *Bolam* is regarded as having decided. But in a significant departure from this view, the House of Lords itself indicated what it expects the doctor to consider in deciding whether or not the proposed sterilisation is in the patient's best interests, and what it will need to be satisfied of before advising that a sterilisation operation may go ahead. The following summary draws on the speeches of Lords Brandon and Goff. The doctor must consider, *inter alia*:

> whether the existing circumstances giving rise to the need for the operation will continue until and unless the operation is performed and no less serious intervention would be appropriate to safeguard the patient's best interests; the opinion, where relevant, of specialist colleagues; the views of the health care team caring for the woman; the special features associated with this operation, namely, the irreversible interference with the reproductive organs of an otherwise healthy person, and consequent deprivation of her right to control her reproduction; the danger of such an operation being carried out for improper motives such as the convenience of others, or being perceived as such; and the fact that to sterilise a woman in these circumstances is a grave decision with considerable social implications.

Here, at last, we have reasoned and articulated guidance on what is a most troubling area. It may not be the guidance which some want or others, such as the Canadians in *Re Eve*,[30] have adopted. But it meets that most important of criteria; it allows for the accountability of professionals pursuant to certain stated grounds. Ultimately, of course, the doctor or the team is left with a judgement to make, but this is both inevitable and desirable as general principles are applied to concrete circumstances. But the doctor's judgement is to be made within the four corners of a set of stated public policy goals.

The welcome (and hitherto unusual) lead shown by the court was taken a step further soon after by the Official Solicitor, the person who the House of Lords indicated should represent the interests of any female whom it is proposed to sterilise. The Official Solicitor issued what he called a Practice Note.[31] (The precise status of such an utterance is unclear, but it serves at least to give helpful guidance.) In this Practice Note the Official Solicitor indicated formally the matters which he would need to be satisfied on before agreeing to a proposed sterilisation. They represent an extensive list of the factors we have already identified. Indeed, they come very close to the kind of checklist which human rights lawyers and specialists in mental health law had been seeking for some time. They represent a public policy position which says that while non-consensual sterilisation is not forbidden it may only be carried out in circumstances of the most serious scrutiny. But, more important for our purposes, they represent a happy conjunction of law followed by guidelines which together recognise the need for sound public policy and respond to it.

Re C[32]   The case of *Re C* is by contrast a disappointment. It arose in the following way. Baby C was born prematurely with severe brain damage caused by a particularly acute form of hydrocephalus, added to which the structure of the brain was poorly formed. The question arose as to the appropriate treatment for the baby and the extent to which the medical team should seek to prolong what an expert had described as a 'hopeless' existence. Put another way, should Baby C receive treatment appropriate to a child who was not handicapped or treatment appropriate to her condition? The question in precise analytical terms was, what in law was the extent of the doctors duty to the child. The case is important because we only have two cases in English law which offer any sort of guidance on the duty of a doctor to a severely handicapped baby, *R* v *Arthur*[33] and *Re B* (1981).[34] Neither of these cases takes us very far, although *Re B* does appear to suggest that it is legally permissible in certain circumstances to allow a severely handicapped baby to die by refraining from carrying out medical procedures which would be indicated if the baby were not so severely handicapped. What the Court of Appeal in *Re B* did not do, and it is not surprising since they had only an hour's notice of the case, is to indicate what the circumstances are which would justify such conduct. Put in terms of the duty of the doctor, the court failed to spell out in anything like enough detail the circumstances under which the doctor could depart from the duty to preserve life. In terms of public policy, this has meant that in an area as critical as the life or death of a child, a most regrettable uncertainty still prevails. It also has the consequence that the task of holding the doctor to account for actions taken in the management of the child is made very difficult indeed.

Re C presented the courts, therefore, with an opportunity to clarify the law and establish reasoned and appropriate public policy. Mr Justice Ward attempted to do so at first instance. He recognised that the child's position was hopeless. It seems clear, however, and this is important for what follows, that Ward J did not regard the child as dying. It would, of course, die without proper nutrition, which the insertion of a naso-gastric tube – the subject of the case – would deliver. But otherwise Ward J seemed to regard the baby as having a hopeless prognosis, i.e. it had no future in terms of any quality of life. This is not the same as saying that the baby is dying. Ward J decided that the naso-gastric tube need not, as a matter of law, be inserted, i.e. the doctor's duty did not extend to preserving life at all costs, if that life was hopeless. At one stage he used the term 'treat to die'. Although less preferable than 'treat for dying', at least this recognised that morally the death of the child was an acceptable aim and outcome. Unfortunately, it was seen by some as smacking of euthanasia and Ward J in a revised judgement gave leave 'to treat the ward in such a way that she may end her life and die peacefully with the greatest of dignity and the least of pain, suffering and distress'.[35]

If *Re C* had stopped there it would have been of some, albeit limited, assistance in developing appropriate public policy in this searingly difficult area. But Ward J's decision was appealed to the Court of Appeal. In the Court of Appeal, Lord Donaldson MR analysed the case entirely on the factual assumption that the baby was dying. This seems, with respect, to be wholly unjustified on the facts. Our understanding is that the baby had no real future but could be fed and otherwise cared for. If it were, there was no reson why it should die. The real question, the one addressed by Ward J, concerned the nature of the doctor's duty in such a case. This is the hard question on which guidance is sorely needed.

By contrast, the question of the doctor's duty to a patient, baby or adult, who is dying is far less difficult to answer. The doctor cannot prevent death. All that can be done is to make the patient comfortable. Admittedly, problems exist at the edges. The doctor may not kill but may administer that which he knows may kill, if he intends thereby to relieve pain. This is relatively well-trodden ground, in the literature if not in case law. F y approaching the case, therefore, as if it were a case of a dying baby, Lord Donaldson MR simply made the more difficult question go away. Sadly an opportunity was missed to formulate clearer public policy. The price to be paid is continued uncertainty in the minds of those caring for severely handicapped babies. The price to be paid is also the continued risk of another doctor or nurse being arraigned, as was Dr Arthur, on criminal charges. A worse way of making public policy could hardly be imagined.

Wilsher v. Essex AHA[36]   The final case to which we wish to refer is *Wilsher*, decided in 1988 by the House of Lords. The point we wish to highlight does not appear in the decision of the House of Lords but rather in the judgement of Browne-Wilkinson VC in the Court of Appeal.[37] We highlight it here for its importance both generally and in the context of our theme, because it has largely gone unnoticed and because Mustill LJ was moved to return to the point later in the case of *Bull* v. *Devon AHA*.[38]

In *Wilsher*, one of the many issues at stake was, who was the responsible party if the child had indeed been harmed by careless conduct? Among the candidates for liability was the hospital (in the form of the health authority). The assumption would, of course, be made that the hospital's liability would be vicarious, i.e. it would be liable for the negligence of its employees, the doctors. An alternative form of liability, however, is primary liability, i.e. the hospital is liable not because of the failings of others but because of its own failings. It is this latter form of liability which we wish to consider here. In the Court of Appeal, Browne-Wilkinson VC commented that no case had been found in which the primary liability of a hospital (health authority) had been considered by the courts. This did not deter him, however, from devoting some time to the point. Even though he did not specifically decide it, he clearly put down a marker that it was by no means clear that a hospital was immune from primary liability in all circumstances and that in certain circumstances, for example those that arose in the case and which we will consider shortly, a future court could well find a hospital primarily liable. He stated:

> 'In my judgement a Health Authority which so conducts its hospital that it fails to provide doctors of sufficient skill and experience to give the treatment offered at the hospital may be directly liable to the patient. Although we were told that no case has ever been decided on this ground and that it is not the practice to formulate claims in this way, I can see no reason why the Health Authority should not be so liable if its organisation is at fault.'[39]

In *Bull*, Mustill LJ, who had chosen not to examine the point in *Wilsher*, decided to echo Browne-Wilkinson VC's warning without again specifically reaching a decision. In discussing the defendant's response, Mustill LJ states:

> 'The second suggested answer was on these lines: that hospitals such as the Devon and Exeter were in the dilemma of having to supply a maternity service, and yet not disposing of sufficient manpower to provide immediate cover, the more so since the small number of consultants and registrars had to deal with three different sites. They could not be expected to do more than their best, allocating their limited resources as favourably as possible.
>
> Again, I have some reservations about this contention, which are not allayed by the submission that hospital medicine is a public service. So it is, but there are other public services in respect of which it is not necessarily an answer to allegations of unsafety that there were insufficient resources to enable the administrators to do everything which they would like to do. I do not for a moment suggest that public medicine is precisely analogous to other public services, but there is perhaps a danger in assuming that it is completely *sui generis*, and that it is necessarily a complete answer to say that even if the system in any hospital was unsatisfactory, it was no more unsatisfactory than those in force elsewhere.
>
> It is, however, unnecessary to go further into these matters, which raise important issues of social policy, which the courts may one day have to address.'

So, what is the point at issue? We will state it here in general terms rather than by reference to the specific facts of *Wilsher*, since our view is that it is a point of wide significance. A patient treated in a National Health Service hospital claims damages alleging harm caused by a doctor's negligence. The alleged facts are that the doctor who treated the patient was inadequately trained or not qualified to carry out the procedure which caused the patient's harm, or did not have the equipment which it is agreed was required but chose to proceed in any event. The health authority concede that there was a breach of the standard of care required of the doctor (and hence of them). They argue, by way of defence, however, that whatever is decided about the liability of the doctor (and hence of them vicariously) they should not be held primarily

liable because the breach was the direct result of a lack of resources, whether of personnel or of equipment. They simply do not
have, they say, the wherewithal to meet the standard which they
agree is the commonly accepted norm. Their choice, they say, it to
close down or do their best, fully aware that their best is below par.
In choosing to do the latter, they argue, they should not be held
liable in negligence since it is a commonplace that the NHS is
under-resourced in very many respects and it is accepted (indeed
expected) that they will press on, hoping that nothing will go
wrong. When it does, and a patient is harmed, the fault lies with the
system, not with them.

The internal logic of this argument, in the context of the tort of
negligence is unconvincing. Certainly, their Lordships were unpersuaded. A defendant agrees that a course of conduct fails to meet
the standard of care required by law. The defendant none the less
proceeds and harms a patient. Stopping there, it would seem to be
indisputable that the defendant, in our case the health authority, is
liable. The defendant then says that he should be excused as he
could not do better because of external factors. The logic of the
tort of negligence has no time for such an excuse. Liability would
seem to follow.

The implications of such a conclusion, if it were the law, are
obvious. One scenario, by no means fanciful, would be as follows.
Hospital managers up and down the country would look at the
services on offer and measure the standard of care that they can
provide against the accepted norm, an exclusively clinical abstract
and often idealised norm of care arrived at without regard, for
instance, to the availability of resources. All services which ran the
risk of operating below par would be withdrawn, after no doubt
acrimonious meetings with the lawyer and finance director. They
would both have raised the spectre of financial disaster as a consequence of multiple negligence suits once lawyers advising plain-
tiffs cotton on to the new ruling, that working below par is *ipso
facto* negligence. The hospital manager aghast at this prospect
might argue, (he or she has studied law!) that patients know that
NHS hospitals have to cut corners and accept this. Furthermore,
they could be reminded of this whenever they presented for
treatment. Would not this make the defence of voluntary assumption of risk available? The health authority's lawyer would probably
respond that if the patient does not have a real choice, i.e. it is
treatment at this hospital or no treatment at all with all that this

implies, then a court could well say that such a patient hardly *consents* in any real sense to receiving below par treatment and consequently can hardly be called a volunteer.

Let us analyse this state of affairs in terms of public policy. If the hint dropped rather loudly by their Lordships becomes law, the court, in effect, would be entering the business of allocating resources in health care. The court would be taking to itself the task of determining how resources should be allocated by the simple expedient of deciding that under-allocation, as determined by the exclusively clinical norm of what is appropriate, is negligence. This would be a staggering development. Resource allocation is an extraordinarily complex issue and one which has been traditionally regarded as non-justiciable. Macro-economic decisions about resources for health rather than, for instance, education have been regarded as proper only for politicians. Meso-economic decisions in health care, determining whether resources go, for example, to the care of the elderly or neonates again have largely been deemed to be political. Micro-economic decisions, determining, for example, which patient gets what share of available care have largely been deemed to be clinical judgements, although this assumption has not passed without comment.

It is a truism in health care that while demand is virtually infinite, supply is greatly limited. It is equally true that the process of allocating resources among competing claims and payments is not only politically sensitive but requires a very great deal of information and expertise. What, we ask, therefore, can a court bring to this process? Judges are neither appointed by nor responsible to the public, and are thereby outside the political process. Judges have no access to the necessary expertise and information. What they have available is whatever the haphazard circumstances of a particular case may bring to their attention. That it will at best be limited is to understate the case. Yet here are two senior judges showing a willingness to exercise judicial power, the power effectively to legislate on health care resources.

The question of public policy raised affects not only the role of the courts in medical law. It has the widest of constitutional implications, going to the very root of the debate about what is for Parliament and what is for the court. Of course, their Lordships may have wanted no more than to put politicians on notice that the courts considered that matters were less than satisfactory in the

Health Service. Yet even this modest aim arguably takes them outside the mainstream of opinion about the proper role of the judiciary. If their aim was larger, it is at best provocative. As we have seen, the making of public policy depends in part on an answer to the question of who is to make it. It has been our thesis that the courts have found themselves forced to do so simply because issues have been brought to them. How far the courts should go, how restrained they should be, what criteria should govern the limits of their public policy making are questions which are inevitably raised by their Lordships' observations. Clear answers will only be given when the larger and more profound issues involved in making public policy are properly addressed.

Conclusion

What do we conclude from this general review? It must be clear that if there is to be any real intention to take seriously the issues we have referred to (and the very many more we could have mentioned), there will have to be a considerable improvement on what is done at present. The courts, no doubt, will continue to try their best, but few will doubt that they are wholly unsuited to the task. Parliament is the obvious institution to look to. It should not surprise anyone, however, that politicians keep their heads down, given the moral complexity of the issues involved.

Surely, the creation of a national commission is the perfect solution for Parliament. Not only is it the correct response to the problems posed. It also allows Parliament to appear to act decisively and creatively, while deferring the hard work and consequent hard arguing to an apolitical body charged with reporting and advising. Once a report is made on any particular matter, the government of the day can avoid some of the more critical opprobrium any recommendations may attract by saying it is merely acting on the best available advice. This will not, of course, make all the problems go away. Parliament cannot avoid its responsibility to decide. But, it would be a major step forward. It would create an atmosphere in which coherent and consistent policy could emerge as a consequence of careful analysis. For that reason alone, perhaps, apart from all the others, it is destined never to appear. Muddling through is still too treasured a part of the British way of life.

Notes and references

1. See, for example, A. Grubb, 'Medical law', in *All ER Annual Review 1989* (London: Butterworths, 1990); J. V. McHale, 'Confidentiality, an Absolute Obligation', *Modern Law Review*, vol. 52 (1989) p. 715; M. Mulholland, 'Neonatal Care and Treatment – The Doctor's Dilemma', *Professional Negligence*. vol. 5 (1989) p. 109.
2. *Report of the Committee of Inquiry into Human fertilisation and embryology*, Cmnd 9314 (London: HMSO, 1984).
3. *Review of the Guidance of the Research Use of Fetuses and Fetal Material*, Cmnd 762 (London: HMSO, 1989).
4. I. Kennedy, *The Unmasking of Medicine* (London: Granada, 1983) p. 120.
5. M. Warnock, 'A National Ethics Committee', *British Medical Journal*, vol. 297 (1988) p. 1626.
6. President's Commission for the Study of Ethical Problems in Medicine and Biomedical and Behavioural Research. For a list of the work of the Commission, see the President's Commission, *Summing Up* (Washington: US Government Printing Office, 1983).
7. On these European developments, see, *Bulletin*, I.M.E. June 1988, pp. 13–20.
8. Australian National Bioethics Consultative Committee, established in 1988.
9. The Biomedical Ethics Board and Biomedical Ethics Advisory Committee were established by the Health Research Extension Act, 1985. Progress has been dogged by political in-fighting in Congress, see A. Capron, 'Bioethics on the Congressional Agenda', *Hastings Center Report*, vol. 19 (1989) p. 22.
10. *Re F (Mental Patient: Sterilisation)*. [1989] 2WLR 1025.
11. Janet Radcliffe-Richards, 'What Price Personal Choice', *The Daily Telegraph* February 8, 1989.
12 The guidelines are administered by the MRC's creation, the Voluntary Licensing Authority, subsequently the Interim Licensing Authority, established in 1985.
13. The Human Fertilisation and Embryology Bill.
14. See clause 11.
15. See, *Review of the Guidance*.
16. See, *Draft Guidelines for Local Research Ethics Committees*, (London: Department of Health, 1989).
17. [1982] 2 All ER 298, 310–11, *per* Lord Scarman. Lord Edmund-Davies was unpersuaded, *ibid.* 308.
18. *Gillick* v. *West Norfolk and Wisbech AHA* [1985] All ER 402.
19. *Sidaway* v. *Board of Governors of the Bethlem Royal Hospital* [1985] 1 All ER 643.
20. *Re F (Mental Patient: Sterilisation)*. [1989] 2 WLR 1025.
21. Ibid., 1039, *per* Lord Donaldson MR (Court of Appeal).
22. '[T]he duty is fulfilled if the doctor acts in accordance with a practice *rightly* accepted as proper by a body of skilled and experienced

medical men', *per* Lord Donaldson MR, [1984] 1 All ER 1018, 1028 (Court of Appeal) (our emphasis).

23. *Re F (Mental Patient: Sterilisation)*. [1989] 2 WLR 1025.
24. *Re B (a minor) (wardship: sterilisation)* [1987] 2 ER 206.
25. *per* Lords Bridge, Brandon and Goff.
26. *per* Lord Griffiths.
27. *Bolam* v. *Friern Hospital Management Committee* [1957] 2 All ER 118.
28. Ibid. 122, *per* McNair J.
29. *Re F (Mental Patient: Sterilisation)*. [1989] 2 WLR 1025.
30. *Re Eve* (1981) 115 DLR (3d) 283.
31. 'Practice Note (Official Solicitor: Sterilisation)' *New Law Journal*, 13 October 1989.
32. *Re C (a minor) (wardship: medical treatment)* [1989] 2 All ER 782.
33. *The Times*, 5 November 1981.
34. *Re B (a minor) (wardship: medical treatment)* [1981] 1 WLR 1421.
35. *Re C (a minor) (wardship: medical treatment)* [1989] 2 All ER 787, *per* Ward J.
36. [1988] 1 All ER 871.
37. [1986] 3 All ER 801, 832.
38. Unreported.
39. *Wilsher v. Essex AHA* [1986] 3 All ER 833.

AIDS: some civil liberty implications

Sarah Spencer

Since AIDS was first identified in the early 1980s, the spread of the disease has been dramatic. In May 1988, the World Health Organization had been informed of 92,000 cases from 139 countries, but estimated that unreported cases would bring that figure to 150,000. It believes there to be between 5 and 10 million individuals who have contracted the HIV infection, of whom 500,000 are in Europe. In the USA, the prospect of one quarter of a million Americans dying of AIDS by the end of 1991 is seen as a cautious estimate.

In the United Kingdom, current estimates of those infected with HIV, the virus which causes AIDS, vary between 20,000 and 250,000. What is known for certain is that, by the end of January 1989, 2049 individuals had contracted AIDS, of whom 1089 have died. Of those who have died in this country, 885 were homosexual or bisexual; 84 were haemophiliac; 37 intravenous drug users and 9 were children who had been infected by a parent.

The threat posed by AIDS, in this country and throughout the world, needs no further emphasis. Faced with a disease which is fatal, for which there is as yet no vaccine and no known cure, politicians and members of the public worldwide have called for extreme measures, violating the human rights of those with HIV or AIDS, in the belief that such measures will help to curb the spread of the disease. The rights of the individual, we are told, must be sacrificed to protect the rest of the community.

The true position is very different. In reality, as the World Health Organization,[1] the Council of Europe[2] and all those dealing daily with those affected by HIV argue, protecting the human rights and dignity of those who are infected is central to the effectiveness of the one strategy which at present has any hope of curbing the spread of the disease: the strategy of prevention.

A successful prevention campaign depends on the authorities having accurate knowledge about the spread of the virus, and imparting that knowledge to the public. It depends on those who are infected, or fear they might be, feeling free to seek advice and confide in those who can provide it. An AIDS prevention campaign cannot, therefore, be effective in an atmosphere of ignorance, intolerance and prejudice. It cannot be effective where the response to those who come forward is hostility, discrimination and breaches of confidentiality about their HIV status. Regrettably, it is just such intolerance and discrimination which many of those with HIV or AIDS have experienced, and which others, as a consequence, fear.

The extreme measures implemented in some countries, and considered in others, fuel these fears: for instance, enforcing immigration controls against anyone with HIV, including denying foreign students access to study; compulsory testing for HIV; compulsory sex cards confirming (in theory) freedom from infection; compulsory tests before obtaining a marriage licence; tattoos to identify those affected; quarantine for those affected or, another proposal, a sort of quarantine in which one retains one's freedom as long as one does not marry, take a job or travel.

One can immediately appreciate why these measures are unnecessary and impractical, as well as unacceptable, when one knows a few basic facts about the virus. The crucial fact is that, while the virus is infectious, its infectivity is relatively low. It is only transmitted by very limited means – essentially by sexual intercourse (including anal intercourse), shared needles and the transfer of infected blood (including transfer to a fetus via the placenta). It is not transmitted by casual social contacts. It is therefore unnecessary to treat it like a contagious disease which, through casual social contact, can be transferred from one person to another. Secondly, it does not follow that everyone infected by HIV will develop AIDS. It may take many, many years for someone with the infection to contract AIDS; they may never do so. It is therefore not only unnecessary, but quite impractical, to keep them in forced isolation.

Thirdly, the test normally used detects the antibodies to the virus, not the virus itself. It can take up to three or four months for the antibodies to develop, and possibly longer. It is therefore perfectly possible for an individual to have a test and for it to prove negative, while the person is already infected but has not yet produced sufficient antibodies to be detected by the test. In those cirumstances, compulsory testing would lead to many people being wrongly assured that they were seronegative (that is, being told they did not have the virus when in fact they did have it). The tests would have to be redone every three months, and new cards issued every three months, for the results to have any validity. Meanwhile, some of those mistakenly assured that they did not have the virus would act accordingly, ignoring the need to stick to 'safer sex'.

It is in the absence of clear, factual information that fear and prejudice spread. The respected Panos Institute, which has done much to draw attention to the effect of AIDS worldwide, puts the problem thus:

> The first epidemic is one of silent infection by HIV, often completely unnoticed. The second, after a delay of several years, is the epidemic of AIDS itself . . . The third is the epidemic of social, cultural, economic and political reactions to AIDS, which is also worldwide, and as central to the global AIDS challenge as the disease itself.[3]

Panos note that throughout the world there is a tendency to blame those with HIV or AIDS for their condition. With the exception of children and haemophiliacs, they are seen to have brought it upon themselves. Panos argue that this tendency 'springs from irrational and xenophobic tendencies which seem to lie deep in the human psyche. Historically, these gut reactions of suspicion and hatred against strangers and minorities tend to show themselves in times of crisis and fear such as AIDS had provoked', as when Jews were blamed for the black death in the fourteenth century. Whatever the reason, throughout the world Panos detect the same pattern: Americans blame Haitians, heterosexuals blame gays, whites blame blacks, Africans blame Europeans.[4]

This approach enables people to feel confident that it will not affect them. It only affects gays, junkies, foreigners, blacks, Europeans, Hispanics – not me or my family. In reality, if one is looking for a pattern worldwide, AIDS is increasingly becoming a disease of the poor who have less access to health education, health care and medicines, less access to condoms, and in general a poorer state of health. Certainly, there is little to be gained from a perspective which focuses on the source of the virus in a particular community, or seeks to apportion blame. We should take a lead from President Kaunda, whose own son died of AIDS, when he says that we must focus not on where AIDS came from, but on where it is going.

Where is it going in the United Kingdom? In October 1988, at the Conservative Party Conference, there was a group of people calling for the introduction of compulsory identity cards so that those issued to people with HIV or AIDS could be marked with a large cross. Some months previously, a national newspaper was prevented only by the intervention of the courts from using information from confidential hospital records to name two doctors with AIDS. There have been examples of individuals with HIV being refused entry to the country and calls for their exclusion, and of people with HIV being removed from their jobs, losing their homes and in one case having their house burnt down. Doctors and dentists have refused to treat patients with HIV; some teachers have demanded that doctors should breach confidentiality so that they can know if a pupil has the infection.

In countries abroad, the examples are often more extreme. The UN High Commission for Refugees is concerned that we may soon see the creation of a new category of HIV-positive refugees who will be unable to find a country which will accept them. The Panos Institute asks whether we are in the process of creating a new class of global sub-citizen who, because they are HIV-positive, cannot travel abroad to work or study, cannot gain refuge from war or political persecution, and cannot get housing or life insurance, jobs or promotion.

Our immediate responsibility is to ensure that these scenarios are not realised in the United Kingdom. To that end I would like to consider three of the areas which have proved controversial: HIV testing, whether it should be compulsory or voluntary; whether doctors should protect the confidentiality of their patient's HIV status; and the treatment of employees who are HIV-positive, or have AIDS. In each case I shall suggest that protecting the civil rights of the individual, far from being a luxury we cannot afford, is entirely compatible with, and indeed essential to, an effective AIDS prevention programme.

Testing without consent

There are three principle issues relating to testing. First, whether we should all be tested compulsorily; the implication being that some decisions could therefore be taken about those people found to be HIV-positive. Secondly, an unrelated issue, whether doctors should be allowed to test their patients without their knowledge or consent in order to protect themselves from possible infection. Thirdly, whether tests can be carried out, anonymously, on blood already taken for other purposes, in order to assist research into the spread of the disease and plan the provision of health care and counselling.

Compulsory testing would require the forcible removal of blood from those who resisted and is unequivocally rejected by both the WHO and Council of Europe.[5] The test would not be being carried out in the individual's interests, and would thus contravene the ethics of the doctor who carried it out. It would also be prohibitively expensive, the pre-test counselling alone being estimated to cost £40 per person. Moreover, given what we know about the test, no action could be taken on the basis of a negative test which would have to be re-done every three months.

Doctors and health care professionals, however, have been much less clear about the correct position to adopt in relation to their carrying out the test on their own patients without consent. In 1987, the British Medical Association's annual conference passed a resolution stating that HIV testing should be at the discretion of the doctor. While the BMA leadership later argued that this meant discretion 'in the interests of the patient', no one had any illusions that this had been the intention of the delegates at the conference. The decision was one based on fear that they themselves could be vulnerable to infection, despite the fact that the risk to health professionals who have been accidentally exposed to HIV infection is low, has been shown to be very remote, statistically some 0.4 per cent according to the Medical Defence Union.[6] The BMA leaders quickly sought counsel's opinion on the legality of testing without consent and found that it could constitute an assult, and the doctors later reversed their conference decision.

Some doctors had argued that the HIV test is no different from any other which they carry out, for which implied consent is often considered sufficient. This argument is misguided. The HIV test is different because a positive result has such a profound effect on individuals' lives. Not only do they have to live with the knowledge that there is a strong likelihood that they will contract a fatal disease; they face social stigma, rejection and discrimination. They can no longer obtain life assurance to protect their dependants.

They may feel they have to end their sexual relationship with their partner, or be given no choice. One survey has shown that people with HIV are 500 times more likely to commit suicide than people of a similar age who are not infected. The HIV test cannot, in these circumstances, be considered routine.

Because of these implications of a positive result, counselling before and after the test is considered crucial. If a doctor carries out the test without seeking consent, he or she cannot provide the pre-test counselling which is needed. When the doctor learns that the result is positive, the patient must then be informed not only of this fact, but also that the test was carried out without consent. In those circumstances, the likely hostile reaction received will not be conducive to providing the kind of counselling which is then needed. Nor will the patient be likely to trust any doctors from whom assistance is needed in the future. Crucially, the doctor has denied the patient the right to decide for him or herself whether he or she wants to have the test done. Many consider it, and decide against. That should be their right.

The British Medical Association,[7] and the General Medical Council[8] are all now clear that it would be unethical for a doctor to carry out an HIV test secretly without the patient's consent. They also advise that it is not necessary, as doctors should always carry out infection control procedures. HIV, is, after all, far less infectious than, say, the more prevalent hepatitis B.

The third issue is whether it is legitimate for laboratory staff to test blood which has been taken for other purposes, not in order to find out if a particular individual is infected, but to find out more about the prevalence of the virus in the population. This practice is known as 'anonymous prevalence screening' and the government announced its intention to introduce it in November 1988. There is a case for saying that, on balance, this is acceptable if the procedure is genuinely anonymous so that no negative consequences follow for individuals from their blood being tested. Undoubtedly their control over their own body is being undermined but this, it has been argued, is justified by the use to which the information can be put to save lives. The key questions are whether the limited information provided really is of central importance, and whether the tests are truly anonymous.

Proponents of anonymous prevalence screening argue that the information can be used to check the spread of the virus between different groups in society in order to plan health care and health education. By increasing understanding of the epidemiology of the infection, it can facilitate the provision of accurate, adequate and realistic public health information, targeted at the right people. It makes it possible to assess the effectiveness of the health education programmes and provides facts which can be used to correct false assumptions and combat prejudice. With accurate projections, the authorities can plan the provision of counselling and hospital beds. Such resource implications are important when the cost of caring for a person with AIDS, over their lifetime, is calculated at £27,000.

Those who oppose the test argue that the limited information which an anonymous test can provide is of little value. Now that life-prolonging treatments are becoming available, they also question the ethics of testing an individual for the virus but not informing him or her of a positive result. Doubt has also been cast on the extent to which it will be possible to keep the test anonymous. Where an individual who is HIV-positive visits a clinic regularly, for instance, his or her test result would distort the statistics in that area. It could therefore be necessary for the clinic to record on a patient's file that the test had been performed in order to avoid further testing. This could affect a future application for life assurance.

Confidentiality

When we turn to the question of confidentiality of test results and related information, we find apparent conflicts of interest which again need to be resolved in favour of the individual whose privacy is at stake, in all but the most exceptional cases. Strong arguments have been made that confidentiality should be breached to protect the safety of health workers, the profitability of insurance companies and the safety of various groups, for example in the case of prisoners, of fellow prisoners and prison staff. Most persuasively, the doctor, it is argued, may have to breach confidentiality to inform the patient's sexual partner.

The opposing argument is that it is only an absolute guarantee of confidentiality which will ensure that an individual who suspects he or she may have the virus, will seek assistance. This concern is borne out by a leaflet published by the Terrence Higgins Trust providing advice on whether or not to have the test.[9] 'Once the test is done' it says 'you may lose control of what happens to the result. Consider before you have it done whether the benefits are worth the risks. Discuss confidentiality with the doctor doing the test.' A study of AIDS patients, reported in the *British Medical Journal*, revealed that the main reason why patients preferred to visit a hospital rather than be in the care of their GP was confidentiality.[10] A second study showed that over 60% of university students were unwilling for their GP to be informed about the outcome of an HIV test carried out at a separate clinic because of concern that the information would not be kept confidential.[11]

It has been argued that such clinics should inform general practitioners as GPs may otherwise make the wrong diagnosis if the patient presents symptoms which are in fact AIDS related. Equally they could fail to take appropriate safety precautions when examining the patient or carrying out minor surgery. The opposing view is that the clinic should explain to the individual the risk that a wrong diagnosis could be made. The doctor should take safety precautions for all patients, some of whom could, unknowingly, be HIV-positive or indeed have hepatitis B or some other infection. The balance is surely in favour of informing the GP only with the consent of the individual. Without such a guarantee, some will fail to come forward for help and thus not receive the advice which could prevent further spread of the infection.

The unexpected onset of AIDS fatalities, and the projected number of such deaths in future, has hit insurance companies and led to significant changes in their policies and premiums. The Association of British Insurers recommends that all men seeking insurance cover of over £150,000 should be required to take an HIV test; while all single men seeking over £75,000 should be asked to complete a questionnaire about their lifestyle. Almost all insurance companies in Britain offering life assurance (or life-based policies) will refuse to cover anyone who is known to be HIV-positive. In this context, some companies have sought to obtain information about sexual orientation and lifestyle from doctors, who have received requests such as the following: 'We would like you to find out in the course of discreet questioning whether this person is homosexual and, in further discreet questioning, whether or not he is promiscuous.'[12] Some companies are also supplying doctors with pre-packed HIV testing kits to be returned to private laboratories which pass the results directly to the insurance company. The British Medical Association rightly objects to both practices.

The issue raises the key question of consent. When individuals apply for insurance, they give a general consent to their doctor providing information about them. If the insurance company requires an individual to take an HIV test, he will ask his doctor to carry out that test. In neither case does this amount to informed consent. The BMA rightly advises doctors that, to carry out the test without counselling the individual on its implications, before and after the test, would be unethical. Likewise, the doctor should only provide information on, for instance, sexual orientation, with the individual's consent, in the absence of which the form should be returned incomplete.

The most difficult question on confidentiality surely arises for a doctor if a patient who is HIV-positive refuses to inform his or her sexual partner. If the doctor stays silent, the partner may become infected. If he informs the partner, fears about confidentiality will be reinforced and more harm could be done in the long term because those who fear they have the virus do not seek assistance. The National Council for Civil Liberties has come to the view that, in balancing these conflicting civil liberties, doctors should in the most extreme circumstances be able to breach confidentiality, but only in such circumstances. An example would be of a man, HIV-positive, who is having regular intercourse with a woman and refuses to disclose that he has the virus. He refuses to wear a condom and the doctor knows, because the woman is also his patient, that she only takes the pill intermittently. She is therefore at risk of contracting the virus and, should she become pregnant, of passing it on to her child.

In such circumstances the doctor should put the safety of the woman and of the unborn child before the privacy of the man and accept the risk that, as a result, others will shun medical help. In practice, were a doctor to breach confidentiality in that way, he could be sued for breach of confidentiality under the common law. In those circumstances, he could argue that he did so in the public interest. The courts have yet to decide such a case. The American Civil Liberties Union argues that doctors should be able to breach confidentiality only *after* a court hearing. Certainly, there is a case for providing statutory protection for the confidentiality of information about HIV and AIDS status, as is the case in Belgium. One should remember that, once the partner has been informed, he or she is not confined by a strong code of medical ethics from revealing that information to others.

Discrimination

Discrimination on grounds of disease status is as iniquitous as discrimination on the basis of any other irrelevant criteria. Despite the good practice recommended by the Department of Employment, however, there are cases where employers are requiring all new employees to undergo HIV screening, and of employees who have lost their jobs as a result of the HIV status becoming known. There is no anti-discrimination law to prevent this happening. In most of the discrimination cases of which we are aware, the individuals have decided against going to an industrial tribunal because of fears of publicity and consequent further discrimination.

Yet such discriminatory practices are entirely unnecessary because of the very limited way in which the virus is spread. The WHO is emphatic that there is no evidence at all that the virus can be spread by insects, food, water, sneezing, coughing, toilets, urine, swimming pools, sweat, tears, shared eating or drinking utensils, protective clothing or telephones.[13] Very few jobs involve contact with the body fluids which can transmit the infection, so most employees are not at any risk. There is therefore a very limited need for anyone to know if any employee is seropositive, and thus no need for screening of new employees, unless it can be shown that the infection or illness will directly affect job performance.

The Terrence Higgins Trust leaflet on taking the HIV test advises, 'Do NOT tell your employer.'[14] Until employees are free from fear of discrimination at work, such advice will remain. In those few circumstances where it would be desirable for colleagues to know of an individuals' HIV status for their own protection, the individual may not risk informing them. That climate of fear must be removed. To do so the advice of the WHO should be taken. Workers with HIV should be treated like any other workers. Workers with AIDS should be treated like any other workers with an illness. It must be clearly explained that there is no risk from working alongside someone who is infected. Employees who will come into contact with people who are infected as part of their work must, of course, be given relevant training.

Employers have already come under pressure, from employees fearful of catching the virus, to redeploy or dismiss the individual concerned. In some cases they have succumbed. In the absence of specific legislation making such discrimination unlawful, it is open to an industrial tribunal to consider such a dismissal fair because it felt that the employer was acting reasonably to protect the profitability of the business. However, such a finding should be rare because the employer must first show that he or she has done all that is reasonably practicable to defuse concern and avoid dismissing the employee.

Conclusion

In conclusion, may I simply reiterate that protecting the human rights and dignity of those affected by the virus is not only essential to protect the quality of life of people who already have a great burden to bear. It is essential to ensure the effectiveness of the health programmes which can limit the numbers of those affected. The effectiveness of those education programmes are, in turn, essential, if we are to avoid a parallel epidemic of prejudice and fear, rooted in ignorance.

The preventive programmes will only be effective if individuals are convinced that a positive HIV test will not lead to breaches in confidentiality or discrimination; or worse, in the future, to quarantine or restrictions on their freedom to travel. If such confidence were felt, resistance to testing and counselling would diminish. To that end, not only must the extreme, impractical and unacceptable proposals be rejected, but we must also look to strengthening the present law to make discrimination unlawful and to give confidentiality statutory protection. These are practical steps that could be taken now to protect the civil rights of those who have the virus, and also to protect the rest of the population who do not.

Notes and references

1. Global Programme on AIDS. Statement from the Consultation on AIDS and the workplace. Geneva. 27–29 June 1988 WHO/GPA/INF/88.7.
2. See Council of Europe Committee of Ministers Recommendation No. R(89)14 to Member States on the ethical issues of HIV infection in the health care and social settings. 24 October 1989.
3. Panos Dossier, 'AIDS and The Third World' (London: Panos Institute, 1988) p. 69.
4. Speech by Panos representative to 'AIDS and Human Rights,' a press conference organised by UK AIDS VIGIL, 25 January 1988.
5. For example, see Council of Europe Committee of Ministers Recommendation No. R(87)25 to Member States concerning a common European Public Health policy to fight the Acquired Immunodeficiency Syndrome (AIDS). 26 November 1987.

6. *AIDS. Medico–Legal Advice* (Medical Defence Union, 1988) p. 3.
7. For example, see BMA Foundation for AIDS Parliamentary Fact Sheet No. 1 (8 December 1988) which is based on the policy adopted by the BMA at its AGM earlier in that year.
8. *HIV Infection and AIDS: The Ethical Considerations*, May 1988.
9. *HIV Antibody: To test or not to test?* 4th edition, December 1986.
10. *British Medical Journal*, Vol. 297 (1988) 16 July.
11. *Journal of the Royal College of General Practitioners* (1987).
12. *The Guardian* (6 July 1988).
13. See Footnote 1.
14. See Footnote 9.

Resource allocation in the National Health Service[1]

Caroline Miles

Introduction

The government's White Paper, 'Working for Patients',[2] is a well laid out document, looking more like a product of management consultancy than the White Papers of old. But its bland appearance is misleading. It is not yet another exercise in reforming and renaming structures, but a revolutionary manifesto. Revolutions are about turning attitudes and perceptions upside down, and that is what the government's proposals aim to do. It is short on prescriptive detail, but manifestos usually are. Some detail has been supplied in the working papers,[3] now available, but they are still very open-ended, inviting responses and ideas for implementation from those of us actively involved in providing health services, whether directly as doctors, nurses and other health care professionals, or indirectly as maintenance workers, medical secretaries, managers and chairmen.

This reluctance to tell everybody exactly what to do is one unusual feature of the proposals. Clearly it is making many people in the service feel anxious. I attended the great national TV show in London at the end of January 1989, and what was striking was the number of questions from the audience about when guidance and circulars would be issued, and the genuine puzzlement caused by the reply from Kenneth Clarke, the Secretary of State for Health, that there would not be any. This has turned out to be not quite true, as experienced Whitehall-watchers predicted. It is only fair to say, however, that the tone of the many documents that have been issued is on the whole more 'managerial' and less prescriptive than the old-style circulars.

The fundamental change introduced by the White Paper, and the one I want to concentrate on, is the proposed revolution in the method of resource allocation in the NHS. In order to grasp just how big a shift in thinking is implied it is useful to set the attempt to introduce market mechanisms in a broad historical context, going right back to 1948. If at times my potted history is sweeping in the manner of *1066 and All That*, I hope that any historians present will make allowances for the need to summarise 40 years in a few paragraphs.

Historical perspective

In the beginning, the main objective of the NHS was to spread the provision of primary care services more evenly, both geographically and in terms of ability (or lack of it) to pay. Hence the decision to make the service free at the point of delivery, and the focus on general practice. While it is a bit of a caricature to say that Beveridge thought that the demand for health care was finite, and the small group of people who turned the concept of a national health service into a reality realised that there was a backlog of existing unmet demand that might cause difficulties to begin with, it is, I think, fair to say that money was not seen as a central problem. The Treasury soon began to feel otherwise, and the first charges were introduced.

A secondary, but not insignificant, objective of establishing a national health service was to prevent the already bankrupt voluntary hospitals (mainly sited in London, the other major conurbations and the old county towns) from final collapse. To begin with, not much attention was paid to the hospital sector, but bit by bit, as the country moved out of the difficult post-war years into the more prosperous late 1950s and 1960s, the focus of concern shifted towards the hospitals, and successive governments supported a large construction programme aimed at achieving a better geographical distribution of secondary and tertiary referral services. These were also the years of new universities and new medical schools. Money was still not the central problem, although the NHS's capital programme, like all government capital programmes, tended to get squeezed and delayed in times of financial crisis. But revenue to the expanding hospital service continued to increase, and primary care services were not restricted to any significant extent. Then came the 1970s, and the introduction of cash limits. From now on, funding issues were uppermost. At the same time the push for greater equity in provision was maintained, and this meant, inevitably in relation to the way the service was administered, ever more centralisation and direction. The notorious Resource Allocation Working Party formula was devised to assist the holders of the moneybags in determining the distribution of the rations. The planning system grew ever more number-crunchingly didactic. Districts, areas and even regions had less and less scope for flexibility in provision and forward planning, and the political battles got noisier and more bitter.

I have said nothing about structural reorganisations in all this, and nor do I propose to. They are largely irrelevant to my theme, except in as much as the more complicated and bureaucratic the structure got, the greater the potential for acrimonious and time-wasting message and data passing, up and down, to no good purpose. Roy Griffiths' 1983 inquiry[4] must be mentioned here, not for its admirable suggestions about management – which now, at last, may begin to be put into effect – but for a paragraph on page 13 dealing with cost improvements. 'It is almost a denial of the management process' he wrote, 'to argue that the modest levels of cost improvement at present required of the NHS are unachievable without impacting seriously on the level of services.'

By the winter of 1987–8, this dictum, as applied to the Hospitals and Community Health Services sector of the NHS, had grown into a burden that had nearly broken the camel's back. With all respect to Sir Roy, while what he wrote is perfectly reasonable in theory, he, and even more the ministers and civil servants who seized on his remark with glee, seriously underestimated the inertia of the system, the size of the managerial task and the steepness of the learning curve up which eveybody working in the NHS – administrators, doctors, nurses – would have to move in preparing themselves to tackle it.

The NHS's ability to cut its costs year after year was assumed in determining allocations, largely by the simple Treasury device of increasing the annual vote by about 1% less than the anticipated rate of inflation. On top of this, health authorities were required to plan for annual 'cash releasing' cost improvements. And so the service arrived at the 1987 autumn of discontent, with closed wards being shown on TV daily, growing waiting lists, horror stories (some of them true) of psychiatric patients being pushed out on to the street as the hospital demolition contractors moved in behind them, and so on. Extra money was found to prop up the service temporarily, while a major review led by the Prime Minister got under way.

The market as a resource allocation mechanism

In considering the White Paper I do not want to dwell on what he leaves out, most notably the whole question of how care in the community is to be funded and managed. The important point to be made is that in the end care in the community is, so far as it has a health component, an integral part of the whole. It is impossible to plan hospital care services for elderly people or for people with a mental illness, without providing for their health care needs after discharge. The new 'purchasing' health authorities will no doubt want to satisfy themselves that the hospitals are making proper arrangements, and not just banging the door after their departing patients. Whoever is made responsible for managing the funds available for care in the community, health authorities and local authorities will need to work together to plan care for individual people requiring it – the chronically ill and handicapped of any age.[5]

The fundamental principle on which the reform proposals for general practice, hospital and community services, self-governing trusts and funding arrangements are built is that the market is better at allocating resources than is a centralised, top-down, provider-led planning system. Separating responsibility for purchasing health care from responsibility for providing it is the common theme linking new GP contracts, GP practices as budget-holders, health authorities as purchasers, and hospitals and other groups of suppliers as providers, whether or not they choose to set themselves up as self-governing trusts.

One way of introducing market mechanisms into health care would have been to adopt insurance-based funding arrangements. There are a number of ways that this could have been done, of which the multiplicity of insurance schemes devised to meet health care costs in the United States is but one, and one that is generally agreed to be unsatisfactory both in relation to matching provision to need and in containing costs. Canada and France, to cite two examples, both have national compulsory insurance systems that combine equity of access with individual choice.[6] The government has, however, explicitly rejected the insurance principle and decided to stick with a service that is largely centrally funded and largely free at the point of delivery, and that even where it is not (e.g. prescriptions, dentistry, eye tests) is subject to flat charges that are not insurable. The White Paper is a bold experiment, which may or may not work, in shifting the weight of responsibility for deciding how the fixed cash resources provided by central government are to be spent away from the providers towards the users of the service, without abandoning tight central financial control. Kenneth Clarke has repeatedly said that he is not assuming that the present level of expenditure is necessarily 'right'. This is not the place to go into the argument over how much real additional funding the NHS has had in recent years, i.e. after taking into account the actual impact of inflation. It seems clear, however, that the immediate question mark over the proposals is whether they will make the present rationing system more flexible, not whether they will make hard choices unnecessary.

In the next section I consider the possible impact of the proposals, and their chances of success in achieving this aim. But before coming on to these matters I want to examine briefly the functions of markets, and their relevance to health care.

A market is a meeting-point of buyers and sellers. The proposals for encouraging large family-doctor practices to hold and disburse their own budgets, and to turn health authorities into purchasing organisations, create the buyers. These buyers will be encouraged to look beyond their own local providers if they think they can purchase better value-for-money services elsewhere, though the scope for shopping around may be limited outside London and other large conurbations such as Birmingham and the West Midlands. The sellers of the future will be the hospitals and community health service organisations, i.e. health visitors and district nurses, ambulance services, and doctors and others performing public health and community care functions. They will be required to enter into contractual arrangements with purchasers of health care whether or not they opt for self-government with the NHS.

To get the market going − think of Monopoly® − the players need a currency with which to deal. Here, the proposal is that the annual total NHS funding will be distributed by the Department of Health to regions and through them to districts on a capitation basis, with some allowance for age structure and morbidity, but in a much simpler and less distorting way than RAWP. Regions will be strongly discouraged from 'top-slicing' large amounts of money to pay for specialised services and fund new developments. It will be up to the providers, such as the teaching hospitals, to 'sell' their specialist services to their own and other district health authorities. All districts will be required to purchase adequate specialist hospital services (e.g. cardiac surgery, neurosurgery) for their populations, as well as general hospital and community services. A start is to be made next year, though the shift to the new formula will take several years to complete. Thus the buyers will start level – more or less – and the distribution of supply will be determined by where they place their contracts.

Such, in very broad outline, is the resource allocation system proposed in the White Paper. I do not propose to go into the details of the self-governing option, or of the invitation to larger practices (those with more than 11,000 patients) to turn themselves into *quasi* health maintenance organisations. Nor can I, in the space available, say anything about the proposals for capital accounting and depreciation policy, which are also likely to have a profound and far-reaching impact on the planning of service provision.

Instead, I want to conclude with some reflections on effects of the proposals in practice. What is the underlying aim, and will they achieve it?

The impact of reform

In thinking about the potential impact of the proposals, and in considering the extent to which they may be expected to achieve their declared aim, it is useful to bear in mind a distinction between the government's intentions regarding implementation and what is likely to happen in practice.

The title of the White Paper is 'Working for Patients', and in her forward the Prime Minister sums up the objective of the proposals in a sentence:

> We aim to extend patient choice, to delegate responsibility to where the services are provided and to secure best value for money.

Why is it necessary to go to all this trouble in order to improve the system of resource allocation in the NHS? Isn't more cash all that is required to make the present problems go away, as many objectors to any tampering with things as they are would have us believe? Let us look across the Atlantic for a minute. Americans, on average, spend 10–11 per cent of their annual incomes on health care, compared with about 6 per cent here. Their incomes are, of course, considerably bigger than ours to start with. Surely they can't have problems of lack of access to care, rationing of scarce treatments, etc? But they do, partly because of the complexity of their health care financing systems and accompanying gross inequalities in access to the most basic health care, but partly, too, because even in the United States the resources are insufficient to provide all the health care that is clinically feasible and offers the prospect of a good outcome – transplant surgery, for example.

Nearer home, many other European countries spend a rather greater percentage of their higher average incomes on health care than we do. In many respects, the provision is better, but not universally so. When it comes to simple measures of good health – life-spans, infant mortality, morbidity from various diseases, etc. – we score higher than many similarly advanced countries on some indicators and worse on others, notably morbidity and death from heart and vascular diseases.[7] However, the reasons for the differences appear to be primarily linked to social conditions and dietary habits rather than to health care expenditure. On the evidence it is difficult to sustain the argument that an increase in the NHS budget of, say, 1 per cent of GNP would result in a comparable increase in the health of the population.

My point is not that there are not obvious deficiencies and gaps in health services. There certainly are, in both the acute sector and in the health care available for chronically ill and disabled people. But at present nobody really knows the extent to which the present NHS budget is being used to maximum effect, or, to put it the other way round, what the unmet needs are, to what extent the obvious shortcomings of the service arise from maldistribution and maladministration of resources, and where the shoe really pinches. Implementation of the White Paper's proposals will point up the areas of the service where more cash is needed and could be spent to good purpose, though it should be borne in mind that, to be put to work, cash must be used to buy resources, and that the service's ability to recruit staff may be a more serious constraint than cash in future years.

I am convinced that the new approach to resource allocation can be made to work to create a more responsive and better overall quality of national health service. Everything, however, depends on the willingness and ability of the people concerned with buying services – the new DHAs and large general practices – and the providers, whether self-governing trusts or still under DHA supervision – to develop rational measures of health care needs, outcomes and value for money, and to deal with each other in a considered and sensible way. The best value for money is not necessarily the cheapest per hospital bed per day, or per course of treatment in hospital if that needs to be followed by out-patient treatment or care in the community, but the best value overall in relation to the patient's needs and achievement of the best possible outcome. This cannot be said too often.

Where willingness and competence are concerned, the omens are mixed. A widespread initial reaction to the proposals from the health care professions and others has been expressions of moral outrage at the very idea that health care has an economic dimension, let alone that there is a 'market' for it. But the NHS spends more than £25 billion a year, and is the largest employer in the country. Like it or not, it is a major sector of the economy, operating at present with only rather vague notions of what it is achieving, and whether or not it could improve outomes by allocating its resources differently. It is, in fact, a classic example of a monopoly, and, as with any other monopoly, it seems reasonable enough, in the public interest, to ask whether the customers – all of us who need health care at one time or another – are getting value for money or not. We should remain agnostic on this point until we know rather more, but it is difficult to maintain the argument that the NHS will perform better if those responsible for providing health care decline to share responsibility for the management of the national resources available – whatever the size of the pool of resources may be.

Much is being said about the cost and difficulty of generating the management information required. The principle of unripe time is a useful fallback position for those who do not want things to change anyway. It is true that the elaborate costing systems developed under the resource management initiative are expensive. It is also true, and perhaps more important, that it takes time to plan and set up systems that are useful in practice. A local Oxford initiative, outside the Management Board's national pilot, has taken a good three years to get to the point of 'going live', even though it started with an enthusiastic clinical team who had in fact already set up their own mini-system, and were fully committed to the concept. One moral to be drawn from this experiment is that involvement and commitment of health care professionals – the people who actually deliver services – is essential. Only they can ensure that the contractual arrangements are realistic and can be delivered.

Provided that both buyers and suppliers are committed to making it work sensibly, the new resource allocation mechanism may be expected to improve the volume of health care that can be delivered for a given cash sum. With the additional proviso that the buyers demand value for money rather than (necessarily) minimum cost, average quality should also improve. That it will automatically and immediately lead to increased customer choice is questionable. Initially there may well be less, or at least appear to be less. Virtually all access to hospital-based consultants and specialist services is controlled by general practitioners, who at present are free to send any patient anywhere, without regard to cost, indeed without even needing to find out what the cost is. This unrestricted choice will disappear when health authorities start contracting with each other, and with self-governing trusts and the private sector, for the supply of services. General practitioners holding their own budgets will be able to decide for themselves where they want to send their patients, and to negotiate contracts with supplying hospitals: others will need to persuade their local health authority to place a contract with a neighbouring district or a self-governing hospital, if they consider that their patients would receive better treatment outside their district of residence. A considerable number of non-budget-holding general practitioners, especially in urban areas divided into a large number of districts, such as London and Birmingham, may find their referral patterns more restricted. But the extent to which these patterns reflect considered decisions about quality, as distinct from ingrained custom and practice, is not clear, and from the point of view of patients there may well be an improvement in the quality and timeliness of hospital care. It seems likely that the legislation to be enacted will, *inter alia*, make it easier for patients to change their general practitioner than it is at present, thus increasing choice at the level of primary care.

Conclusion

I have restricted myself to a consideration of resource allocation in the NHS. Even so, there are several aspects of the topic that I can only touch on.

One is the extent to which increased competition among service providers will become a reality, and whether, if it does, it will work for the benefit of the system as a whole. Here, it seems to me, the potential for competition – whether on a straight price or a value-for-money basis – will inevitably vary in different parts of the country. In London, and other large urban conurbations, competition could arise, though whether the less successful will be allowed to go to the wall is another matter. In the rest of the country, however, its impact is likely to be much more limited, simply because potential competitors are so much further apart. GPs in the frontier territory will have a choice, as indeed they have at present. As money begins to flow with patients their choices will affect the size of hospital budgets. But transport costs alone, setting aside the wishes of patients and existing working relationships between GPs and hospital consultant staff, make mass transfers between Plymouth and Teesside, or even between Oxford and Birmingham, an unlikely prospect.

Another aspect of resource allocation that I have not touched on at all is the funding of teaching and research. There are some sensible noises about this in the White Paper, but no firm indications of future policy as yet. What seems clear is that whoever disburses the funds – and it appears that Sir Christopher France's inter-departmental committee may recommend that this responsibility should pass from the Department of Education and Science to the Department of Health – medical schools will have to make contractual arrangements with the hospitals providing teaching facilities.

Clinical research imposes substantial costs on the hospitals where it is carried out, a cost that has not hitherto been properly recognised and funded by the NHS, despite its general duty to support research. A study recently carried out for the Department of Health in Oxford (not yet published) has estimated the costs at a minimum of 1 per cent of the district health authority's budget, a significant percentage in relation to the general development addition of rather less than 1 per cent p.a. that the authority has received in recent years. The Academic Medicine Group, in a recent statement, has urged the separate funding of clinical research,[8] and this would appear to be foreshadowed in the White Paper.

There are two concluding points that I would like to make. The first has to do with management. In discussing resource budgeting and contractual arrangements I focused on the key role and responsibilities of doctors and other health care professionals. In the past four years, since general management was introduced to the NHS following Griffiths, shifts in attitudes and perceptions have begun to happen amongst them, and amongst all other, non-clinical, staff working in the NHS. But there is a very long way to go. One must question whether the implications of the radical changes in methods of resource allocation set out in the White Paper are as yet clearly understood by managers, let alone by the health care professionals. It is, in fact, impossible to be sure how they will work in practice until they are tried. Hence the argument for experiments in limited areas. But while pilot experiments in self-governing hospitals and budget-holding general practices are possible – and indeed envisaged in the White Paper, with its talk of the 'first wave' – payments will need to follow patients nationally or not at all. They will inevitably be based on quite crude estimates to begin with, but even that should be an improvement on the present lagged annual adjustments between regions.

Finally, in keeping to my brief I am conscious of appearing to ignore the special characteristics of the relationship between doctors and other health care professionals, on the one hand, and the patients seeking their help, on the other: the (varying) mix of anxiety, trust, paternalism and autonomy. Not so: I am acutely aware that good medical practice depends on good relationships between the clinical community, amongst whom I include the professional managers, as well as doctors, nurses, paramedical staff, laboratory and support staff, and their clients. Medical audit is concerned with improving practice, and a comprehensive medical audit process includes a consideration of how the professionals use the resources available to them, including their own and their colleagues' time and skills. It is unfortunate, and sadly misleading, that debates about the problems of the NHS are so often reduced to arguments about the cash, instead of focusing on how to make better use of the human and material resources that are available now and any additional resources that more cash could buy. The

NHS's clients have good reason to expect that those entrusted with the use of those resources will handle them in a professional and responsible manner.

Notes and references

1. This lecture was delivered in March 1989. At that time only the outline of the government's proposals for the reform of the NHS was visible. Throughout the following summer the future of the service – or in some eyes its imminent demise – was never far from the headlines, thanks mainly to the BMA's campaign. Sadly, the public debate generated more heat than light. Most of what has been written or said has reinforced my perception of the White Paper as initiating a revolution in attitudes towards the purchasing and supply of health care, a bold attempt to break away from a producer-determined rationing system without abandoning the principle of free access.

   Faced with the choice between rewriting the lecture to take account of new nuances and details, or leaving it largely as delivered, with minimal additions and alterations, I have opted for the latter course. At the editor's request I have slightly expanded the discussion of the market as a resource allocation mechanism in the third section. Otherwise I have limited myself to correcting or amending facts, in the light of later information, and to adding a few references to material published since March 1989.

2. The Secretaries of State for Health, Wales, Northern Ireland and Scotland: *Working for Patients*, Cmnd 555 (London: HMSO, 1989).

3. The following ten Working Papers have been issued so far (all obtainable from HMSO): 'Self-governing Hospitals'; 'Funding and Contracts for Hospital Services'; 'Practice Budgets for General Medical Practitioners'; 'Indicative Prescribing Budgets for General Medical Practitioners'; 'Capital Charges'; 'Medical Audit'; 'NHS Consultants: Appointments, Contracts and Distinction Awards'; 'Implications for Family Practitioner Committees'; 'Capital Charges Funding Issues'; 'Education and Training'.

4. The results of this inquiry were issued in the form of a letter dated 6 October 1983 from Mr Roy Griffiths (as he then was) to the Secretary of State for Social Services, Norman Fowler MP.

5. The government's plans for the future of community services to meet both health care and social needs have now been published in *Caring for People*, Cmnd 849 (London: HMSO, 1989). As expected, the primary responsibility for organising social care will remain with local authorities, which will, however, be required to focus on developing individual client packages and procuring the necessary services, rather than providing many of the services (e.g. residential homes) themselves, as they do at present. Health authorities will continue to provide 'mainstream' community services, including district nursing, and will be expected to work closely with local authorities in planning client packages and ensuring that they are delivered.

6. Among recent comparative studies, Mark W. Field (ed.), *Success and Crisis in National Health Systems* (New York and London: Routledge, 1989) is useful, with good bibliographies. It includes a chapter on the Soviet health system. The recent House of Commons Social Services Committee Report *Resourcing the National Health Service: the Government's Plans for the future of the National Health Service*, ref. no. 214–111 (London: HMSO, 1989, includes some comparisons with the French and Dutch systems, but concentrates on the iniquities and inequities of the American system, which is of limited relevance to the White Paper proposals.

7. See Field (ed.) *Success and Crisis*, p. 266, for a summary of recent data for four countries, including the UK and the USA.

8. The Academic Medicine Group 'Academic Medicine, Problems and Solutions' *British Medical Journal*, vol. 298 (1989) pp. 573–9.

Homicide, medical ethics and the principle of double effect

Peter Byrne

Introduction

In medical practice, decisions are taken which bring in their wake the hastening of death or the shortening of life. Medical ethics, therefore, is necessarily concerned with the ethics of homicide. Some medical acts appear to be homicidal in their thrust, so we must know when such acts are licit and when not. The principle of double effect is relevant to this task because it has something important to say about when we can choose to perform a clinical act which has death as one of its consquences, and because it offers to tell us something about which acts are to be classed as homicides.

The principle can be formulated in different ways. It is concerned with the licitness of acts which produce both good and bad effects, when in normal circumstances (that is in the absence of any special justification or mitigation) the bad effect would be such as to make the act illicit and preclude its being done. According to a typical formulation of the principle one can perform an act which has both good and bad effects if: the act in itself is not bad, its bad effect is not intended and is not a means to its good effect, and the good effect is proportionate to its bad effect.[1] Crucial to the principle as formulated are a number of ideas which are peculiar to non-consequentialist forms of moral thought. One is the notion that it matters what the inherent quality of an act is and that this is determined by what is intended in it. From this flows the thought that a bad effect which is intended is at the least more difficult to justify than one that is not intended. It therefore adds to the mitigation or justification of an act which has a bad effect to show that the effect in question is not intended and thus not part of the act itself. Since homicidal effects are particularly weighty and hard to justify, and since to say that an act has the quality of being a homicide is normally to say that it is wrong, the principle of double effect is of particular importance in the ethics of homicide. It points to an area of mitigation or justification for acts which are in part homicidal in their thrust that may be of crucial importance in deciding when they are licit.

Such extra ground of justification for acts which have homicidal effects is not required by a consequentialist ethics of homicide. At its crudest it will tell us that a homicidal act is licit if whatever good effects it produces are proportionate to its evil effect of bringing about the death of a human being. A consequentialist ethics can broaden the notion of justified homicide to the extent that it needs no reliance on extra areas of mitigation, especially if it contends that bringing about the death of a human being is not in itself an evil effect of action. Consequentialists typically argue that human life is valuable only in so far as it occasions other valuable things (such as the exercise of rational autonomy). A great many human lives (particularly among infants, the irreversibly comatose or senile) are then of no value and taking them is not an evil, other things being equal. The consequentialist attacks the use of the principle of double effect on the very ground that it narrows the sphere of licit homicide too far. Or, he attacks the non-consequentialist ethics of homicide for its alleged inconsistency: first it wants to say that something more than proportionate good is required to justify homicide; later, nothing that this would narrow the scope for performing many acts which have good effects, it re-admits the balancing of causing death against good consequences (such as the termination of suffering) by allowing such balancing where death is not intended as part of the act itself.

It appears that in medical ethics we must have a just reckoning of the range of licit acts which are homicidal in their thrust and we must have a consistent ethics of homicide. Consider scope first. Both established clinical practice in this country and agreed principles in medical ethics would wish to exclude general recourse to euthanasia through the deliberate administration of poisons by doctors. Yet both practice and ethics accept that there are many contexts where all technically possible steps should not be taken to keep patients alive, or where measures to relieve suffering should be used even though the hastening of death may be one of their foreseen consequences. The range of acts with homicidal consequences deemed licit is not as narrow as some defenders of the idea that each and every moment of life is of infinite value might suggest, nor as broad as enthusiasts for euthanasia want. Established practice and ethics want to occupy some form of middle ground on the range of licit homicidal acts within medicine (though there is plenty of room for disagreement about specific treatments and policies within this middle ground). The question naturally arises 'Is there any consistent way of demarcating this middle ground?' The consequentialist argues that the principle of double effect is empty and therefore that consequentialist reasoning (simple weighing of good and evil effects) is covertly employed to escape from the narrow position. If this is so, then any broadening of the range of licit homicidal acts cannot coherently stop short of endorsing full-blooded euthanasia.

The wrong of homicide

So far I have written vaguely of consequentialist versus non-consequentialist accounts of the ethics of homicide. There are distinctions to be made between different approaches within both of these schools. Of particular importance for double effect is the distinction between absolutist and non-absolutist conceptions of the wrongness of killing a human being.

By an absolutist conception I refer to one we associate with the traditional formulations of moral theology. This holds that all acts which take innocent human life amount to murder and are illicit, granted only that the taking of such life in intended within the acts in question. 'Innocence' may be defined in the narrow sense of not morally or legally guilty of some serious crime (usually itself a homicide or the intention to commit homicide), or in the broader sense of 'not itself threatening the life or well-being of others'. Absolutists will be forced to adopt the narrow view of the range of licit homicidal acts and rule out the sort of 'midwifery' toward death and the dying common in medical practice and referred to above, unless they can show that such hastening of death or not prolonging of life is to be classed as the production of unintended side-effects of otherwise good acts. The absolutist is one who, by definition, has to rule out simple appeal to proportionality in justifying homicide and so must have recourse to extra justifying or mitigating conditions. An apparent paradox within traditional medical ethics is the great contribution made to it by Roman Catholic moral theology, which has employed the absolutist position on homicide alongside a rather liberal view of the scope of licit acts having hastening of death or not prolonging of life among their consequences.

It is possible to be a non-consequentialist and non-absolutist in the ethics of homicide. We could follow Devine[2] in arguing that acts of homicide are inherently evil and Mitchell[3] in contending that the value of human life flows from the nature of being human. The evil of homicide then depends on the inherent character of homicidal acts: from the fact that they are instances of taking human life. But this is not to say that the value of human life cannot be outweighed and the evil of homicide justified or mitigated by consequences (cf. promise-keeping can be inherently right and promise-breaking inherently wrong, even though it is sometimes right to break a promise in the light of the consequences of keeping it). Acts of homicide are illicit unless justified (hence, the category of murder) but they can sometimes be justified by appeal to necessity. I intend no argumentative force to attach to 'necessity'. It only refers in a summary way to those cases *in extremis* where life may be taken. As well as the character of the one who is killed (non-innocence), non-absolutist, non-consequentialist moralists can also allow under 'necessity' the avoidance of what may be judged wholly unacceptable consequences of continued living for the victim of homicide. The avoidance of otherwise uncontrollable suffering where death is in any event near is an example of the kind of circumstance that a non-absolutist might count as justifying homicide. Common morality would, I think, allow as justified homicide the mercy bullet to the dying soldier on a battlefield for whom no relief from suffering is otherwise available.[4] This is not to say, as contemporary consequentialists hold, that the value of life and the wrongness of killing depend on the quality of the life taken, but rather that quality of life considerations may justify homicide on some extreme occasions.

Non-consequentialists of both persuasions mentioned here make common ground in denying that human life is of value only as the means to other goods, and hence that killing is evil only if it excludes those goods. The value of human life can rest on the worth that each member of the human species has simply by being a member of that species. Religious and non-religious folk will disagree over how they spell out that worth, but a lowest common denominator would be that each member of the species is an instance of personhood. Each is the possessor of a rational nature, even though none of us displays that rational nature throughout our natural lives and in some it is impared throughout their existence.[5,6] Here I endorse what Devine terms the 'species principle' for deciding what acts fall under the opprobrium of homicide: all those which have as their object the death of any member of the human species. It is common for consequentialist moralists to claim that a species principle of this sort commits its user to the confusions, prejudices and unjust discrimination of 'speciesism', making mere membership of the human species the sole criterion for enhanced moral status.[8] This complaint is both logically and morally confused. As I have pointed out elsewhere,[9] the species principle for giving all human beings the protection of restraints on homicide employs membership of the human race as a *sufficient* and not a *necessary* condition for judging the inherent value of a life. Enhanced moral status is not thereby denied to any other creatures of whom we might want to say that they were persons and entitled to the protection personhood demands. The species principle is consistently universalisable. If there are other kinds of creatures who of their nature are rational and autonomous, then all members of such species should be given the protection demanded by the application of the species principle.

The substance of my argument is that there is no good reason to deny that all human beings, regardless of quality of life and attainment of the powers of personhood, should not be seen as inherently valuable, such that, unless special reasons are offered to mitigate or justify, to kill them is to murder. This judgement is, I believe, in line with legal definitions of murder and homicide and with public sentiment. Appeal to personhood, generalised by reference to the species principle, is not the only ground for a non-quality-of-life ethics of homicide. Devine offers other grounds;[10] religious moralists bring in yet further arguments. I have not proved that a non-absolutist but non-consequentialist ethics of homicide is the right one. But I hope to have indicated how it might be plausible.

The non-absolutist agrees with the absolutist over the use of the species principle to demarcate what acts fall into the important moral category of homicide. But he is also inclined to accept that the presumption that no human life is to be taken is in principle rebuttable by reference to the quality of the remaining life left open to a potential victim of homicide. What makes this different from the sole reliance on quality of life considerations characteristic of a consequentialist ethics of homicide? It might appear that the difference between non-absolutism and non-consequentialism is merely a verbal one. They will both reason, by reference to quality of life considerations, that certain lives may be taken, but will dress up this reasoning in different clothes. They may both judge, for example, that malformed babies without any prospect of living a recognisably human existence should be put to death. They are both happy with killing the innocent.

Despite these arguments there is no reason to suppose that abandoning absolutism leads to consequentialism. The fact that the non-absolutist begins from the presumption that to take any human life is wrong does lead to real differences in the conclusions he reaches and the way he is prepared to support them. As we shall see below, he can pay attention, in a way closed to consequentialism, to the manner in which death results from action in judging the licitness of acts which bring death in their wake. Moreover, because he thinks that the general wrongness of homicide reflects a duty not to kill owed to all human beings, he can distinguish between, for example, the morality of killing an infant and the morality of preventing the conception of an infant. A consequentialist ethics of homicide is hard pushed, of course, to make this kind of distinction. It must appeal to indirect considerations to make the difference. It is true that the non-absolutist sees the duty not to kill as defeasible. Facts about the quality of life remaining to potential victims of homicide may allow the duty to be set aside. This will largely be because such facts are relevant to whether other duties, such as those connected with beneficence and non-maleficence and respect for human dignity, are liable to be infringed in drastic ways if action is taken to prolong a life. Yet, because he starts from this universally owed duty not to kill, the non-absolutist puts the onus of proof on those who think it should be waived in any case. Moreoever, the non-absolutist who rejects consequentialism is under no obligation to spell out a positive criterion of what is the minimum quality of life that makes a human life worthy of protection. It is enough for him that we can describe or imagine certain states of misery and degradation which give priority to other duties than those of not killing or prolonging life.

These differences will have real consequences for the way practical decisions are made.[11] If, for example, there is real uncertainty in the prognosis of dreadful suffering or degradation for a patient, then the non-absolutist will tend to give the benefit of doubt to continued life. Some argue that there is an inherent and crippling vagueness in *all* medical judgements about the future quality of life for patients.[12] If this were true, which I do not accept, a typical consequentialist ethics of homicide would be in disarray. Its main ground for making discriminations between licit and illicit homicides in medical practice would have been removed. But the central plank of non-absolutism, the universal though defeasible duty not to kill, would remain untouched.

There are a number of reasons why it is worth outlining the non-absolutist, non-consequentialist approach to homicide when discussing double effect. One is that both defenders and opponents of the cogency of double effect sometimes argue that in choosing to use or abandon double-effect reasoning we are choosing between consequentialist and absolutist ethics in homicide. Matters are much more complicated than that. It is true that if the principle of double effect is completely abandoned as philosophically confused we shall have to abandon absolutism, on pain of embracing an extremely narrow view of the range of licit homicidal acts. For if we give up the principle we shall face greater pressure to admit that judgements of proportionality can be made directly on homicidal acts, something which absolutism denies (claiming that the intended killing of an innocent human being can never be judged licit in the light of expected good). However, the non-consequentialism I favour allows judgements of proportionality to be made even in cases of intended homicide, albeit that they will rarely lead to the justification of homicide.

If abandoning double effect does not lead to consequentialism automatically, it is still the case that the non-consequentialist who is not an absolutist has some, lesser, stake in defending the principle. It is not absolutely vital to him in delimiting the scope of licit homicidal acts in a consistent way, but it may be of some use. For example, scope and consistency may give grounds for supporting the idea that intended, direct killing is especially heinous and thus in need of especially strong arguments from proportionality to justify it. Scope and consistency in applying the ethics of homicide in medicine may give reason to hope for some means of distinguishing the general, though not universal, wrong of euthanasia in clinical practice from the general, though not universal, correctness of the 'midwifery' of death described in the previous section.

In this section we have seen that there is more than one alternative to a consquentialist ethics of killing. Double effect is absolutely vital to an absolutist alternative, for without it absolutism becomes intolerably narrow, leading to the injunction within medical ethics that patients are to be kept alive as long as is technically possible and regardless of their condition. Double effect is useful to the non-absolutist alternative if non-absolutism requires some firm ground for refusing to endorse the general recourse to full-blooded euthanasia in clinical practice (the ground that intended killing is especially heinous). Double effect has, however, come under sustained philosophical criticism of late, criticism which I shall illustrate by points taken from Kuhse,[13] though in fact the weaknesses of the principle of double effect are also visible in recent defences of it.[14] Three criticisms are worth considering: (1) that the application of the principle is hopelessly flawed and inconsistent; (2) that there is no proper distinction between foreseen and intended effects of voluntary actions; (3) that given the elasticity in the way actions and their effects can be described that principle is vacuous. All three criticisms have a common aim; to show that no middle ground on the range of licit homicidal acts is possible – we must choose either the consequentialist's very broad view or the hopelessly narrow view implied by unqualified absolutism.

Direct and indirect killing

Kuhse devotes a great deal of space to showing that, whatever the theory behind double effect, non-consequentialists who write about the ethics of clinical practice produce no consistent account of why the range of licit clinical acts with homicidal consequences should extend in some directions but not in others. Her comments on Roman Catholic treatments of abortion will introduce her point.[15]

Roman Catholic moralists will argue that it is wrong (because it is unjustified homicide) to directly kill an unborn child through termination of a pregnancy, even if one does so with the best of motives, e.g. to ward off some substantial threat to the mother's life or health. But it is not necessarily illicit to indirectly cause the death of a fetus, if termination of pregnancy is the foreseen but unintended side-effect of a licit act. If the mother has cancer of the uterus, which threatens to be fatal if not removed, then the pregnancy may be indirectly terminated through surgery on the uterus. A proportional justification of a homicidal effect is here allowed, provided that the effect is only foreseen and not intended. Kuhse's point is simple: in neither direct nor indirect terminations of a pregnancy is the death of the fetus (assuming this to be homicide) part of the act itself on traditional accounts of double effect. It is not sought as an end in itself and in neither case is the death of the fetus a means to producing the intended result (in case one: the termination of a pregnancy; in case two: the removal of a diseased uterus). No more than in indirect terminations, need the actual death of the fetus in direct terminations be an essential aim of the act. That aim is to end a dangerous pregnancy; the fetus's death is merely a tragic but inevitable consequence of that aim.

These examples raise a number of important questions. In both a death is foreseen and voluntarily brought about. In both the bringing about of that death need not be part of the reason why the act is done. Kuhse is asking us to reflect that if foresight and volition is sufficient in the one case to allow the death as intended, why is it not so in the other? Or, if the death is not wanted as part of one's essential aim in both cases, why can we not say in both that the death is unintended? Her two criticisms of principle are hereby introduced: foresight and volition are sufficient for intentionality, and the flexibility of descriptions of acts and aims reduces double effect to vacuity.

In her commentary on the use of the principle, another type of major criticism of its application emerges. We noted above the tendency of traditional medical ethics to be absolutist yet liberal in the manner in which it allows doctors to refrain from prolonging life at all costs. Kuhse, in relation to a number of cases, brings out the point that this liberality is based on an inconsistent use of double effect. What is directly intended in such acts may be described by traditional moralists as 'not making a patient undergo a burdensome treatment', or characterised in some way that indicates that the relief of suffering is the aim of the act/omission, while the failure to prolong life is merely an unintended side-effect of this way of managing the patient's overall condition. Consider, however, one outline example, that of refusing to treat a secondary infection by routine antibiotics in a patient who is suffering some primary, terminal illness. Most would agree that it is licit not to treat, if by treating a burdensome terminal state were merely prolonged. But what makes treatment burdensome in this instance is the fact that it prolongs life. What makes non-treatment action which avoids needlesss suffering is that it does not prolong a worthless state of being. The hastening of death (or the not prolonging of life) turns out to be part of the means by which the act of omission secures its end. So, by double effect hastening of death is intended[16] (this point is openly acknowledged in the BMA's discussion of euthanasia[18]).

Kuhse hopes by commentary of this sort to show that we cannot avoid using proportionality to allow the licitness of taking some innocent life intentionally. Much non-treatment of the dying in clinical practice can only be viewed as being based on decisions that patients' lives are not worth prolonging and on the opportune use of a non-treatment option to decrease the chances that a patient will live on.

The foreseen and the intentional

It may be that the principle of double effect could be patched up in the face of such criticisms of its actual use. Whatever their ultimate cogency, they at least serve the purpose of introducing the two main objections of principle Kuhse offers of double effect. The first asks if there is any clear account of intention which enables us to say that foreseen effects of acts voluntarily undertaken are yet still unintentional. Elaborations of the principle will say that unintended effects are those not sought either as a means or as an end within an act. But all this seems to indicate is that what is deemed unintentional is not desired in itself or as the means for bringing about something desired in itself. It is something that the agent regards as unwelcome and does not form part of the reason for his action. But if he none the less chooses to bring about this effect as part of some overall package, then in some sense he must want and desire to bring it about; he must think it worth bringing about, all things considered. To call such an effect unintended is to move the ascription of intentions away from the firm ground of the voluntary and the foreseen to the private world of inner acts of intending and wanting. In this world the agent is given free licence to select some aspects of the things he brings about knowingly and freely and call them 'unintended'. Lo and behold: moralists then tell him that he can reason about the licitness of these aspects of his actions differently! In Kuhse's view we might enquire of the agent's reasons and inner desires as a means of fixing his motives for what he did (which will be of some interest if we are concerned with the goodness of agents as well as the rightness of acts), but the character and description of the act he performs is fixed by the foreseen effects of his performance.[18]

We cannot respond to this and other objections of principle to the cogency of double-effect reasoning by appealing to the fact that homicidal consequences of medical commissions for omissions are for the most part very uncertain and remote effects of acts intended primarily to have quite other effects. There is a rough sense in saying that an effect is unintended if it is most uncertain to follow from an act. If a bad effect is a very uncertain consequence of an act, an agent may be excused from the charge of negligence if he brings that effect about unknowingly. Yet certainty and uncertainty do not make the whole difference between the intended and unintended. Many effects actively strived for in action may be uncertain: what we hope and desire to bring about may, after all, be a long shot. What we endeavour to achieve may be uncertain in its realisation. Moreover, homicidal effects of some medical omissions and commissions may be predictable with fair certainty. While uncertainty in outcome is not to be dismissed in the classification of an act as an intentional killing, the critic of double effect is likely to stress the cogent point that once a homicidal effect is seen as a possible outcome of an act, and the act is undertaken none the less, responsibility for that effect is assumed. The agent can then be surely held accountable for its occurrence. The effect must have figured in the agent's deliberations, if it was foreseen at all.

It is not totally correct to make all foreseen effects of voluntary acts intentional. If the free decisions of other agents stand between my act and some of its foreseen effects we would not normally say these effects are part of my act. But leaving aside that kind of case, appeal to foresight and volition can be seen to have great merit as an account of intentional action, a point demonstrated when we consider van den Beld's recent defence of a real distinction between foresight and intention. Van den Beld sets forward the intention of an act as that which is revealed in the reconstruction of the practical reasoning implicit in the act. Reconstructed practical reasoning takes the form of a statement of the agent's desire in acting, what he must do to achieve this desire and, finally, a description of the act he then performs. An effect is unintentional with respect to an agent's action if it finds no place in his practical reasoning. No statement of this effect occurs in the account of the wants which he enacts or in the description of the act which the agent performs to enact these wants.[19] Though this may be an admirable attempt to escape from the privacy and arbitrariness of intentions, it is unsatisfactory on two grounds. In the first place, if an agent foresees that a certain effect wil be brought about by his action, and if he reasons at all about what he does, he must take this effect into account. If it is an undesired effect, but he none the less brings it about, he must reason that it is worth bringing about – all things considered. He then intentionally brings it about. Moreover, it is very odd to say that a freely chosen, foreseen effect is unintentional with respect to the agent's action. For this invites the question 'In what manner is it brought about unintentionally?' By the nature of the case it is not brought about accidentally, unwittingly or inadvertently. But if it is unintentional some such alternative description should apply to it.

Let me press this last point a little further. The principle of double effect does not assert that we are not responsible for unintended effects of otherwise good acts – if it did it would not contain the condition that we must justify unintended effects by proportionality. Freely bringing about the unwanted effect with foresight seems sufficient for responsibility because, surely, it is sufficient for saying the effect is intentionally brought about. I can sometimes be responsible for what I do or allow unintentionally, as in the varied instances of bringing about something negligently. The undesired side-effect is not, however, brought about negligently, as with a culpable omission to foresee and hence forestall something evil. The defender of double effect owes us an account of how the undesired side-effect can be foreseen, be freely opted for, be something for which the agent is responsible and yet still be brought about unintentionally.

Relating this theoretical discussion to a clinical case, consider the example, which figures often in Kuhse's discussion, of the physician treating pain in a terminally ill patient with ever-increasing doses of analgesics. To have the effect of reducing pain the dose now required will be such as to bring the strong likelihood of hastened death. (Developments arising from hospice medicine have now made this example somewhat anachronistic. As Saunders and Bains note 'good pain control throughout a terminal illness makes the use of high-level opioids less likely'[20] (see also Twycross[21]). Hastened death is not desired in itself or as a means within the doctor's action. If the patient's death is not hastened by the analgesic the doctor will not take extra steps designed to kill. He accepts it as an unwelcome consequence of an otherwise good act, sufficiently justified by the good that accompanies it. But he cannot claim that the act is justified overall because the patient's hastened death is unintentionally brought about while it is also true that he clearly foresees its coming about and freely acts so as to bring it about. This probable outcome is secured intentionally, but is justified by the overall good aimed at. We have an act that is homicidal in one of its effects, but which is justified by the good associated with that homicidal effect.

Intended versus intentional

The problem with saying that foreseen side-effects of acts are unintentional is that the agent both believes that these effects will accompany his act and in some sense desires (as part of an overall package) to bring these effects about. If belief plus desire exhaust the meaning of 'intention' then we must conclude that he intends what is called the 'side-effect' just as much as those effects which constitute the reasons for performing the act. However, desire and belief do not exhaust the meaning of 'intention' and there is point in saying that what count as side-effects according to double-effect reasoning are not intended, even though they may be brought about intentionally.

To distinguish between what an agent does having intended it, and what he does intentionally may appear to be straining credulity too far, yet the existence of such a distinction has been cogently argued for by Bratman.[22] The force of saying that I intend a certain outcome is narrower and more specific than that of saying that I bring it about intentionally. Intentions have a number of features which go beyond mere desire and belief and which demarcate what is intended in acts from what intentionally flows from them.

Bratman ties the key features of intentions to the fact that intentions are part of our roles as planning, deliberating agents. Intentions control my acts in a way mere desires do not, and are specially related to reasons for action: they reflect the reasoning behind an act and in themselves provide reasons for contemplating other acts.[23] There are three specific features of what I intend. First, an intention once formed will play a special role in further practical reasoning. It will pose problems for deliberation (precisely what must I do to put it into effect?), as such it will lead to and control means–ends reasoning as the agent works out the appropriate means for enacting the intention. Second, the intention will constrain other intentions and plans of the agent. He will be constrained in planning other things which would be incompatable with giving effect to his intention, and planning for further acts will be based on the premise that what is intended will take place. Third, having an intention to bring an effect about entails endeavouring to bring that effect about. So having that intention means that the agent's act must 'track' that effect. If circumstances change, what the agent does must be adapted so that his actions continue to focus on that bringing about of his intended result.[24]

None of these features will be present in the case of an effect which is merely foreseen and freely chosen as part of the overall result of an agent's intended actions. These points may be illustrated by the examples of the physician who intends to kill a patient through giving him some lethal substance and the physician who knowingly shortens a patient's last days through administration of an analgesic with the intention merely of controlling suffering. If the patient's hastened death in the second case is not intended, but merely foreseen, then this likely outcome of the doctor's act will have played no part in his further practical reasoning. He will not have been posed a problem of deliberation about when and exactly how much analgesic will be needed to secure death and thus death will not have figured in or provoked any means–ends reasoning. The contrary will be true of the first doctor. Having intended the patient's death, the first physician will also have been constrained in planning and doing other things for the patient that might prolong his life. Not so the second physician: his intention is merely to relieve suffering, and if hastened death is truly an unintended consequence of his planning, he may contemplate and reason about further forms of care that may prolong life, provided that they are compatible with the original intention. Finally, the actions and plans of the first doctor will 'track' the outcome of death because he is endeavouring to bring that outcome about, but this will not be true of the second doctor. We then have a distinction between what two agents intend that is not based on private or arbitrary inward acts, but rather on the nature of human beings as planning agents and on the differences in the past, present and future planning and reasoning of the agents concerned. This may be enough for us to say that the two acts in question are different in nature, even though their foreseen consequences are the same.

How an agent may intentionally do what he none the less does not specifically intend to do may easily be explained if Bratman's case is followed thus far. What the agent wants to bring about may have the potential to motivate him to bring about foreseen, but unintended, perhaps unwelcome, consequences of intending that effect. An intention may then have the 'motivational potential' to get the agent to bring about, knowingly and freely, consequences which are not part of his reasons for action and which play no part in shaping the course of his future plans and intentions.[25] Forming and acting on this intention, he then intentionally brings about the attendant side-effects of his action as well as the result he specifically intends.

We are now in a position to see that there is something true and false in each of the treatments of the principle of double effect which provide the starting points for this paper. Kuhse is right to maintain that freely chosen and foreseen consequences of actions which all admit are the responsibility of the agent cannot be set aside as unintentional. She is right therefore in contending that death brought about through such 'side-effects' is intentional death. She is further correct in maintaining that the principle 'Innocent human life is never to be intentionally taken' is either to be abandoned, or retained only at the cost of drastically narrowing the range of licit acts with a homicidal thrust, with important consequences for medical ethics. Yet she is wrong in arguing that, in effect, there is no difference between knowingly and freely bringing something about and having an intention to bring it about. She is therefore wrong in supposing that there is no difference in kind between those acts where death is merely brought about intentionally and those where it is specifically intended. Van den Beld is wrong to maintain that unwelcome but foreseen side effects are unintentional. But he is right to locate the nature of what is intended in the character of an agent's practical reasoning, and thus right to suppose that there is a difference between intended effects of action and merely foreseen effects. The distinction between the intended and the intentional is at the heart of any attempt to sort out recent writing on double effect.

Questions still remain. We have yet to treat of the third main objection in Kuhse to the use of double-effect reasoning in the ethics of homicide (the seeming arbitrariness of distinguishing what is intended from the consequences of our intentions). More important for present purposes is the need to indicate what moral weight, if any, should be attached to the difference between specifically intending someone's death in an act and 'merely' bringing about that death intentionally. The consequentialist could, of course, accept the distinction between the intended and the intentional and contend that it has no moral weight.

Delimiting homicide

What is intentionally done is done freely and knowingly and the agent is responsible for it, albeit that he may none the less not specifically intend it if it is an unwelcome side-effect of his act. Where what is intentionally brought about is the death of a human being, are not these facts sufficient for saying that the agent has killed that person and thus committed a homicide? How could the fact that the death is not intended begin to mitigate or justify the bringing about of death? Only if these questions can be answered satisfactorily can double-effect reasoning be of any use either to a re-phrased version of an absolutist stance on homicide, or a non-absolutist, non-consequentialist ethics. The consequentialist is waiting to be told why we should not simply judge on the proportion between the foreseen consequences of any homicidal act in deciding its licitness.

If I bring about death intentionally without forming and enacting any intention to kill, it still appears to be the case that I kill, and if my killing is unjustified or cannot be mitigated in some way, then I murder. Consider the case of a terrorist whose intention is to blow up some public building but whose act can only be accomplished at the cost of killing bystanders. If the bomber foresees that deaths are the probable outcome of his act, accepts those deaths as tolerable costs of his act, then we will say that he killed (in this case unlawfully and unjustifiably), even though he may have formed no purpose to kill. He still killed, despite the fact that death was a side-effect of his act given his 'self-governing intention' (Bratman's phrase). Should not our reasoning about lawful and justified but unintended homicides follow the same pattern? Murder in English law requires death to be brought about with 'malice aforethought' but a jury may be allowed to infer that someone kills with intent if he acted knowing that death would follow his action in the ordinary course of things, even though he may not have wanted death to follow.[26] This follows from the standard legal definition of intent which has it that a jury may judge an effect to be intended if: it is the actor's purpose, or if it is not the actor's purpose, it is a virtually certain consequence of the act and the actor knows that it is so.[27] Some have argued that the legal latitude given to the definition of killing and intent is confused, departing from the ordinary understanding of intent as what an agent purposes rather than foresees. But the common law notion of intending can be seen, in terms of the analysis defended in this paper, to have preserved the truth that what I freely and knowingly bring about I intentionally bring about. It appears also to have preserved the truth that intentionally bringing something about makes me fully responsible for it, even though I do not want that outcome and it is not part of the reason for the act I perform.

In a case of killing and double effect in medicine, such as the unwanted death of the fetus brought about through removal of a cancerous uterus, the clear-headed conclusion appears to be that intentional taking of life amounts to killing. The doctors in this classic example kill the unborn child while not purposing its death. Yet there is a difference in character between this killing and killing which is intended. The bringing about of death plays no part in guiding the plans and actions of the doctors. The dispositions of thought and action which accompany intentional but unintended killing are different from those which accompany killing which is the outcome of actors' self-governing intentions. One who kills with intent to kill is disposed to reason about what precise means to adopt to bring about death; he is disposed to endeavour to kill and to systematically shape his behaviour so that this endeavour succeeds; he is disposed to base any future plans on the premise that the death of his victims is accomplished and to block such plans as may be incompatible with accomplishing this death.[28] Intended bringing about of death has a different background in human agency from mere intentional bringing about of death. This appears to affect its moral character in two ways. First, the relevant dispositions of thought and action that lie behind it can be viewed as morally evil, other things being equal. Second, this type of bringing about of death can be seen as more fully or directly having the character of killing. On both grounds it could be argued that intentional and intended killing requires greater moral justification than intentional but unintended killing.

Kuhse is inclined to dismiss the background differences in human agency between these two types of killing as matters pertaining to the goodness of agents rather than the rightness of acts and as merely to do with differences in the motives that lie behind acts of killing. She contends that one who, in my terms, kills intentionally but with no intention to kill merely has to kill focusing on the 'right' thoughts (e.g. 'I don't really want this fetus to die, merely to save this woman from cancer').[29] But there is much confusion in this account. The difference in agency between the two types of killing does not reside in what speeches agents recite before action, but in the different structures of practical reasoning and planning that surround what they do. This is not a difference that depends on the whims of agents but on what they try to accomplish and how they reason about that. 'Motive' is the wrong word to describe the disctinctions that result. A physician who kills with lethal poison intending to bring about death may have the same motive, namely to spare a fellow human being from suffering, as one who accepts hastened death as a foreseen side-effect of prescribing a powerful analgesic. This similarity does not alter the difference in agency between the two acts. Put simply: one act is the enactment of a plan to kill, the other is not.

There is, of course, a point about the goodness of agents associated with the difference in agency I describe. Granted that we regard killing as evil unless justified, we regard someone who is prepared to plan and endeavour to kill as more evil, other things being equal, than someone who is only prepared to accept killing as an unwanted side-effect of morally good types of endeavour. The agent who intends to kill is more directly implicated in the evil of killing than the one who does not, because of the relation between this first agent's intentions and the bringing about of death. Now if we allow intention, analysed in terms of practical reasoning and planning, any role in determining the character of the acts an agent performs, then the moral differences suggested by the thoughts about agency developed here are not *simply* a matter of the 'goodness of agents'. An act embedded in the one form of agency (intended and intentional bringing about of death) could be wrong, while an act where death was equally certain as an outcome, but not intended, could be right. The difference in agency gives some ground for the frequent characterisation of intended homicide as 'direct killing' and unintended, but intentional, homicide as 'indirect killing'.[30] This is not because of a difference in the certainty of foreseen death that may accompany these apparently different types of killing, but because direct killing flows from human agency which is reasoning about how best to kill, basing future and present plans on the premise that killing is to be accomplished and endeavouring to kill. Direct killing is more deeply implicated in the evil of killing. (Note: this is not to say that direct killing is always worse than indirect killing. Some direct killing may be justified, if I am correct in this paper. While a terrorist who indirectly kills many, intending merely to destroy property, commits a gross evil, because there is no justification through proportion for what he does and because of the wanton disregard he displays for human life.)

Kuhse sees no difference between direct and indirect killing because she is able to put the important matters of agency concerned on a par, having reduced these to *belief* in the certainty of resulting death (which may be equal) and *desire* (both direct and indirect killers may desire with equal measure the overall packages produced by their acts and which include death). Only trivial differences in what may be before the agent's mind when he acts remain. But to characterise matters thus, we have argued, reflects the confusions about intention and agency Bratman has diagnosed for us.

None of these reflections will be interesting to those who are not concerned with the inherent qualities of actions as opposed to their consequences. No refutation has been offered of the consequentialist who rejects such a concern *in toto* and on general grounds. At most the consistency of a non-consequentialist appeal to the character of agency and acts has been defended: the non-consequentialist does not have to rest his distinctions on sand. Fuller argument will, and does, focus on our intuitive judgements about particular moral cases and on the importance of the constraints on achieving goals that non-consequentialism provides.[31]

Act descriptions

A reformulated principle of double effect claims some difference between the considerations needed to justify a bad effect of an action that is intended and a bad effect that is intentionally brought about but not intended. The third major criticism of the use of double effect to defend a non-consequentialist ethics of homicide to be drawn from Kuhse, contends that it is arbitrary which effects of action are to be described, in our terms, as intentional and intended and which as intentional but not intended. This arbitrariness arises out of the freedom agents have in the description of their actions and intentions. The result is a complete liberty to conclude that an envisaged homicidal result of action is not intended and thus to avoid the more strenuous justification of this result that a non-consequentialist ethic of homicide demands.

This point has already emerged in the discussion of alleged differences in types of abortion. The foreseen death of a fetus resulting from removal of a cancerous uterus may be claimed to be unintended (but not as unintentional), but so equally may the death of a fetus resulting from *any* termination so long as the method used does not rely on killing the fetus as a means to termination. The termination of pregnancy is the result which is the focus of the doctor's planning and practical reasoning and the object of his endeavours. The fetus's death is merely the foreseen, inevitable side-effect of that planned result. To what certain ground may we appeal to limit an agent's liberty to redescribe the intended result of his acts? It cannot be the inevitability of the foreseen result, for intentional but unintended homicidal side-effects may be as certain as intended ones (as the abortion examples illustrate). If certainty of outcome is relied upon, the entire distinction between foresight and intention will collapse. Nor can it be argued that the distinction rests on what is logically entailed by any minimal description of the agent's intended result. If I intend any result only when its occurrence is logically necessary given that I achieve what I purpose, then the realm of side-effects and indirect killing has expanded beyond all proportion. The cannibals who roast a man over a fire, cutting off pieces of juicy flesh as they do so could then claim not to intend the death of their victim, since it is always conceivable that he could, by some miracle, survive their treatment of him. That he die is not logically entailed by the description of what they purpose (to feast on his flesh).

These difficulties in fixing the description of intended results are well illustrated in van den Beld's comments on the example of a craniotomy performed on an unborn child to save the life of its mother in labour:

> But it could now be argued that, strictly speaking, the death of the child is not wanted by the doctor who performs the operation: neither as an end nor yet as a means. What the doctor really wants as a means is the reduction in the size of the head of the child so that it is small enough to pass through the birth canal. Certain operative measures must be taken to make it smaller; though these are measures which will ensure the death of the

child. The upshot of such a presentation of the case is that the death of the child is a foreseen, but not-intended, effect of the operation.[32]

These points about the elasticity of act descriptions may be thought to be of theoretical interest only. Yet it is a fact, as Kuhse notes,[33] that they are actually exploited by writers in medical ethics in the justification of homicidal acts which might otherwise fall under the ban of some absolutist principle of homicide. They appear to point to the conclusion that even the most absolutely certain outcomes of one's intended actions can be accounted unintended if they are not actively desired. Finding an expected result of one's action unwelcome and bringing it about with reluctance become sufficient for saying that the result is unintended and a mere side-effect. But this is absurd. There must have been many people (consider soldiers in battle) who have aimed at and fully intended the deaths of others, yet done so with reluctance and with no active desire for those deaths.

The account of intention we have taken over from Bratman enables us to rule out straightaway relying on active desire or reluctance as the test of what an agent intends. We may see how on his account an agent can fully intend to do something with reluctance when we remind ourselves of the three-fold role that a result that is intended will play in the agency of a rational being. It will pose problems for practical reasons, setting the agent on a course of working out appropriate means to ends. It will constrain his further reasoning and planning, being a premise on which further plans are based and ruling out other possible options. It will finally be something that the agent endeavours to do, so that his reasoning, planning and action will 'track' an outcome that is intended. Inner distaste or reluctance are beside the point. There are two ways of applying the analysis of intention to the problem about act description posed by van den Beld and Kuhse. They allow narrower and broader interpretations of what counts as an intended homicide, and may effect the casuistry of medical ethics accordingly.

On the narrower view, the unborn child's death in the craniotomy example would not count as intended homicide. For the actual death of the fetus does not play the necessary three-fold role in the obstetrician's agency. It is merely the inevitable accompaniment of something that does: reducing the size of the child's skull. The doctor is not set the task of working out exactly what he must do and when to kill the child. The child's death is not the basis and parameter constraining consideration of further practical problems, nor does the doctor endeavour to kill the child. His actions do not 'track' the infant's death; he does not adjust them in the light of changing circumstances to ensure that death results. He does not intend to kill the child.

It is plain that on the narrow reading of the analysis of intention, standard cases of abortion which do not rely on the fetus's death do not count as intending to kill. It might be urged that this is to allow a hopelessly wide latitude to the bringing about of death. The natural thing to say about the craniotomy case and standard instances of abortion is that they are cases where the child/fetus is intentionally killed. But note that the analysis of intention favoured in this paper will allow just that reaction. On a narrow reading of what is strictly *intended*, the deaths of the unborn in these envisaged examples remain *intentional* since they are freely and knowingly (foreseen with great certainty) brought about. It therefore allows such cases to be described as instances of homicide and for the question to be raised of whether they are justified homicides (granted we count the fetus as a human person). Even on the narrow version of what counts as an intended result of action, there is plenty of scope for the criticism of abortion for those who are so minded. The ethical point of refusing to say that in the craniotomy or abortion examples we have intended killing is that they would not then have the apparent additional heinousness of flowing from the type of agency which intends killing. Other things being equal, they would then have the initial degree of mitigation provided by being instances of indirect killing. The grounds of lack of proportion or reckless disregard for human life would remain to be pressed and argued for by those who wish to condemn abortion. What would be declared illegitimate are the manifold attempts of moral theologians, well documented by Kuhse, to distinguish between some foreseen deaths of the unborn as the result of medical interventions as genuine killings or abortions and others as not. Leaving aside the admitted instances where death of the unborn is specifically intended, the only sensible question that remains is: 'Granted that death of the unborn may be brought about in medical practice intentionally for different reasons and in different circumstances, which killings of the unborn are morally justified and which not?'

There is a degree of intuitive appeal in the conclusion that the obstetrician who performs a craniotomy on an unborn child does not intend the child's death. For the foreseen death of the child is not vitally involved in any of the purposes he is enacting. They could be accomplished even though the child by some miracle lived on. But there is also a degree of artificiality in saying that the death is not intended, and this artificiality carries over into the other real and imagined cases described above. It is not merely that in some particular circumstances or even in the normal run of events that crushing a child's head results in its death. As Devine puts if there is no 'non-fantastic scenario' in which the result – crushing its skull – could be achieved without bringing about its death.[34] It is not that aiming at the result of crushing the skull logically entails the child's death; it does not. Rather, in the actual world in which we now live there is no way at aiming at one result without bringing about the other. This is why we need the suppositions of divine intervention (miraculous restoration of the child's cranium) or of science fiction (surgeons in 200 years' time or on Mars could perform a reversible craniotomy) to imagine the one effect occurring without the other. This means that in the real world in which we now live there is no way in which the foreseen result of crushing the child's skull could play the three-fold role that Bratman gives an intention and yet not encompass the child's death. In our actual world the distinction between intending this type of craniotomy while not intending death and intending the craniotomy while also intending death is one to which no difference attaches. As far as practical reason is concerned they are identical. Now, of course, relying on the notion that there is no non-fantastic scenario which will allow us to intend one result without intending another makes what may be strictly intended by one's acts into something that is relative to the state of technology and knowledge – a fact which Kuhse notes and judges adversely.[35] What is fantastic today may become a realistic possibility as human capabilities advance. While this might appear odd, there is a logic in allowing the development of technology to influence the character of what may be intended and what not. Intentions are a function of human beings as planning, practically rational agents. What may be planned and reasoned about practically *does* depend on the state of the world and our capacities as agents in it. There is a particular oddity in the thought that someone's agency in bringing about A and B could be changed to 'intending A while only intentionally bringing about B as a side-effect' from 'intending both A and B' just because, unbeknownst to the agent, we had discovered some non-fantastic scenario in which A could be realised without B. The differences in technical and physical possibility that might effect the joint realisation of certain outcomes have to be routed via the knowledge that is open to the agents concerned.

The broader interpretation of what an agent strictly intends would follow Devine in saying that if there is no non-fantastic scenario in which A can be brought about without B, then one strictly intends to bring about B if one strictly intends to bring about A. In the absence of such a scenario, to plan to do A is, in effect, to plan to do B. The force of adopting this broader interpretation would be to characterise the craniotomy example as one in which death is strictly intended. It would complicate the moral debate about abortion by making the gestational age at which termination is performed something that influences the possible description of the doctor's intention, and therefore of his act. It cannot be maintained that ordinary moral judgement dictates the adoption of either the broader or narrower interpretation of the range of strict intention. Act-descriptions are too fluid in moral discourse for that to be the case. The moral force of describing the obstetrician in the example as intending the death of the child is limited unless we have adopted a new version of the absolutist principle to the effect that one may never licitly *intend* to take innocent life. However, the very fact that such a principle would depend on these debatable matters of judgement in its application makes it dubious as the linchpin of an ethics of homicide. As an intended killing, the doctor's act lacks the initial mitigation of a merely intentional killing, but the morally important features of the case remain the fact that the doctor is faced with an apparently unavoidable choice between lives and does not in any event take life wantonly or recklessly. These will be the main facts in considering the morality of the agency behind the killing that he undertakes.

Acts and omissions

Before attempting to draw together the various threads in this paper one fresh topic needs to be treated. The distinction between acts and omissions is often urged as a major factor in the justification or mitigation of acts with homicidal consequences in medical practice. It is claimed that a reflective medical ethics can rule out euthanasia as illegitimate but permit standard forms of medical practice which hasten or allow death through types of non-treatment, on the grounds that there is an important moral difference between killing and letting die. Causing or hastening death through omission is not killing and does not need to face the kind of justification demanded of acts of homicide (so claims the BMA report on euthanasia of 1988). Since I have summarised the extensive philosophical critique of the killing/letting die distinction elsewhere,[36] I shall only treat it very briefly now.

Any attempt to place great reliance on omission 'letting die' as a mitigating factor in the ethics of homicide faces an initial major difficulty of principle. It is perfectly possible for an omission to have the same intentional relation to a death as an act of commission. I can knowingly and freely bring about someone's death through a series of omissions. I can, through omission, strictly intend a death. I can do so where my inaction in certain circumstances is the outcome of means–ends reasoning about how to kill someone; where his death is a result constraining further reasoning of mine; and where my decisions not to do various things is part of an endeavour to kill that person, 'tracking' his death accordingly. A simple example of the intention to kill through omission would be a parent killing an unwanted infant through a policy of starvation. Death brought about through omission can amount to intentional killing where there is an opportunity to save life and where that opportunity is freely foregone in the knowledge that avoidable death will result. Direct and indirect killing through omission are both then possible and to say that death is the result not of commission but omission is not of itself to remove it from the category of killing.

Because of the possibilities mentioned above, no generalised distinction between killing and letting die can figure in a sound medical ethics. Yet there are cases of foreseen death through omission which do not amount to killing, and so some version of the distinction may be of use in particular cases. A hierarchy of increasing approximations to direct, intended killing through omission in medical practice can be constructed, and only after review of this range of cases can the question of whether letting die in medical practice ever amounts to euthanasia be settled. I have explored this hierarchy previously,[37] and concluded that, at least in areas of paediatric practice, intended killing (in this case of malformed infants) is accepted by some parts of the medical profession. Some alleged letting die in medicine is homicide in the strictest sense and requires the strenuous justification demanded of any example of intended killing.

Conclusion: the sanctity of life

This paper began by raising the question of whether the principle of double effect is of value in determining which acts are homicides and which homicides are licit.

Re-stated after the criticisms of Kuhse have been taken into account it proves of limited value in determining which acts are homicides. For we have seen that some deaths which the principle counts as side-effects are still intentionally brought about. On that ground there is no reason to deny that what are termed 'indirect killings' by some defenders of the principle should not count as killings.

The principle turns out to encapsulate a distinction between intended and intentional foreseen consequences of acts. We have seen that, if one is inclined to admit important deontological, non-consequentialist constraints on action, there is ground for regarding intended killing as in need of greater justification than intentional killing. A distinction of some moral importance between direct and indirect killing re-emerges. However, the re-formulated distinction does not appear to be of great help to an absolutist version of non-consequentialism, but to be best used by a non-absolutism which demands only some much stricter justification of intended killing than of intentional killing.

Absolutism is weakened through critical exploration of double effect because its traditional formulation must be abandoned. It can no longer claim that innocent human life is never to be taken intentionally. The cost of maintaining this claim is a disastrous narrowing of the range of licit acts which have homicidal consequences. No voluntary acts which are foreseen to bring about death will then count as permissible. It appears impossible to have a consistent and humane medical ethics if this restriction is accepted. Even on its traditional, pre-critical formulation the principle of double effect has been shown by Kuhse to be inconsistently and arbitrarily applied in determining which medical procedures leading to death are acceptable and which not. Better to abandon such casuistry and accept that in these problem cases we have intentional killings and look to the proportionate good and harm which results to sort out their permissibility.

Might not an absolutist principle be re-framed along the lines 'It is always wrong to take innocent life where such killing is *intended*'? There are a series of related objections to this way of proceeding. In the first place we have seen in the above that there are real difficulties in drawing a line between intended (direct) and intentional (indirect) killing in many cases. Vagaries surround the correct description of intentions and acts in relation to their consequences. Given that there is no wholly satisfying solution to this problem and that there is a large grey area in the judgement of what counts as direct killing, it seems odd to insist on the absolute wrongness of any intended (direct) killing. Intended killing is worse, other things being equal, than mere intentional killing because of the different nature of the agency behind it. Granted that we regard killing with dread, it seems especially important not to make killing an object of our planning as deliberate agents. But if we are also aware that some deaths will have to be accepted as the intentional results of our acts and that it is difficult, if not arbitrary in some cases, to distinguish between intended and intentional outcomes, it appears more rational to say that an act which has the clear character of an intended killing must bear a particularly heavy weight of justification to be licit. It is indeed difficult to see, short of revelation, how we could be sure that no practical dilemma would present itself in which it would not be right to plan and endeavour to take innocent life.

The non-absolutist regards human life as being of intrinsic worth. He considers that we have a strong duty not to kill. Therefore, in all normal circumstances he will not seek to gain his practical goals through killing. What killing he is prepared to contemplate is that which is the side-effect of actions intended to gain other results. Killing in these cases is not planned. He recognises, however, that there may be extreme circumstances in which it is right to contemplate killing as a goal to be pursued by rational agency. 'Non-innocence' in the victim of homicide (best interpreted as that victim being a grievous threat to others) is but one of the circumstances which might make it right to choose killing as the rational outcome of a pratical problem. But he sees no reason *a priori* why this should be the only circumstance in which killing might be pursued as a goal of action, contending only that other justifying circumstances have sufficient weight to match the general heinousness of killing. We can at least imagine cases in medical practice where sufficient reasons could be found for killing as the best solution to a practical problem and so euthanasia cannot be ruled out on this view. If what has been said in this paper (and by many a recent philosopher) about the severe limitations of any killing/ letting die distinction is right, then there are indeed numerous circumstances in which doctors feel it right to purpose at least the hastening of death through omission, and some cases in paediatric care (and maybe elsewhere) where respected opinion and practice favours purposed killing through omission.

The non-absolutist allows the possibility that the duty not to kill may be overriden by other duties. He cannot, on this ground, agree with the sense which many see in the notion that human life is sacred. Talk of the sanctity of life may be a useful way of highlighting through metaphor the severity of the duty not to kill, but no more.

Notes and references

1. cf. A van den Beld, 'Killing and the Principle of Double Effect', *Scottish Journal of Theology*, vol. 41 no 1, (1988) pp. 93–5.
2. P. E. Devine, *The Ethics of Homicide* (Ithaca: Cornell University Press, 1978) pp. 15–17.
3. B. Mitchell, 'The Value of Human Life', in P. A Byrne (ed.), *Medicine, Medical Ethics and the Value of Life* (Chichester: John Wiley, 1989) pp. 41–2.
4. See P. A Byrne, 'Authority, Social Policy and the Doctor–Patient Relationship', in G. R. Dunstan and E. Shinebourne (eds), *Doctors' Decisions* (Oxford: Oxford University Press, 1989) pp. 235–6.
5. See P. A. Byrne, 'The Moral Status of the Human Embryo', *Nederlands Theologisch Tijdschrift*, vol. 41 (1987) p. 143.
6. Mitchell, 'The Value of Human Life', pp. 43–4.
7. Devine, *The Ethics of Homicide*, pp. 51–60.
8. See, for example, H. Kuhse, *The Sanctity of Life Doctrine in Medicine* (Oxford: Clarendon Press, 1987) pp. 212–3.
9. P. A. Byrne, 'The Ethics of Medical Research', in P. A. Byrne (ed.), *Medicine in Contemporary Society* (London: King's Fund, 1987) pp. 31–2.
10. Devine, *The Ethics of Homicide*, pp. 17ff.
11. cf. Mitchell, 'The Value of Human Life', pp. 42, 45.
12. Linacre Centre, *Euthanasia and Clinical Practice* (London: Linacre Centre, 1982) p. 30.
13. Kuhse, *The Sanctity of Life*.
14. van den Beld, 'Killing and the Principle, pp. 93–116.
15. Kuhse, *The Sanctity of Life* pp. 94ff.
16. Ibid. p. 141.
17. British Medical Association, *Euthanasia* (London: BMA, 1988) p. 35.

18. See Kuhse, *The Sanctity of Life*, p.161.
19. See van den Beld, 'Killing and the Principle', pp. 105–7.
20. C. Saunders and M. Bains, *Living with Dying* (Oxford: Oxford University Press, 1989) p. 17.
21. R. G. Twycross, 'The Relief of Pain', in C. Saunders (ed.), *The Management of Terminal Malignant Disease* (London: Edward Arnold, 1984) pp. 64–90.
22. M. Bratman, *Intentions, Plans and Practical Reason* (Cambridge, Mass.: Harvard University Press, 1987).
23. Ibid., pp. 16–17.
24. Ibid., pp. 141–2.
25. Ibid., pp. 119–20.
26. J. C. Smith and B. Hogan, *Criminal Law* 6th edn (London: Butterworths, 1988) p. 330.
27. Ibid., p. 56.
28. cf. Bratman, *Intentions* p. 154.
29. Kuhse, *The Sanctity of Life*, pp. 160–1.
30. cf. Devine, *The Ethics of Homicide*, pp. 118–19.
31. See van den Beld, 'Killing and the Principle', pp. 93–4, for an indication of the strength of the non-consequentialist's case.
32. Ibid., pp. 108–9.
33. Kuhse, *The Sanctity of Life*, pp. 97ff.
34. Devine, *The Ethics of Homicide*, pp. 122–3.
35. Kuhse, *The Sanctity of Life*, p. 101.
36. P. A. Byrne, 'The BMA on Euthanasia: The Philosopher Versus the Doctor', in Byrne (ed.), *Medicine, Medical Ethics and the Value of Life*, pp. 19–25.
37. Ibid., pp. 15–33.

A woman and her unborn child: rights and responsibilities

Ian Kennedy

What I am concerned with here are the relative rights, if any, of a pregnant woman and her fetus. I am concerned with the question, what should, or must, a woman do, or refrain from doing, while pregnant? I shall seek to examine the issues involved from the point of view both of ethics and law. The latter enquiry will necessitate an examination of whether there is a need to make public policy, and if there is what form that public policy should take. Curiously, although the nature of the problem only has to be stated to see how significant it is, there has been relatively little scholarly comment in the United Kingdom[1] in contrast to the United States.[2]

Some examples

Consider the following.

1. In the case of *Jefferson* v. *Griffin Spalding County Hospital* in 1981, the Supreme Court of Georgia handed down the following judgement.[3]

> On Thursday, January 22nd, 1981 the Griffin Spalding County Hospital Authority petitioned the Superior Court of Butts County for an order authorising it to perform a caesarean section and any necessary blood transfusions upon the defendant, an out-patient resident of Butts County, in the event she presented herself to the hospital for delivery of her unborn child which was due on or about Monday, January 26th.

[The Superior Court found] Defendant is in the thirty-ninth week of pregnancy. In the past few weeks she has presented herself to Griffin Spalding County Hospital for pre-natal care. The examining physician has found and defendant has been advised that she has a complete placenta previa; that the afterbirth is between the baby and the birth canal; that it is virtually impossible that this condition will correct itself prior to delivery; and that it is a 99 per cent certainty that the child cannot survive natural child birth (vaginal delivery). The chances of the defendant surviving vaginal delivery are no better than 50 per cent.

The examining physician is of the opinion that a delivery by caesarean section prior to labor beginning would have an almost 100 per cent chance of preserving the life of the child, along with that of the defendant.

On the basis of religious beliefs, defendant has advised the Hospital that she does not need surgical removal of the child and will not submit to it. Further, she refuses to take any transfusion of blood . . . .

The Hospital . . . seeks authority of the Court to administer to defendant all medical procedures deemed necessary by the attending physician to preserve the life of defendant's unborn child . . . .

The Court has been requested to order defendant to submit to surgery before the natural childbirth process (labor) begins. The Court is reluctant to grant this request and does not do so at this time . . . .

On Friday, January 23, the Georgia Department of Human Resources, acting through the Butts County Department of Family and Children Services, petitioned the Juvenile Court of Butts County for temporary custody of the unborn child, alleging that the child was a deprived child without proper parental care necessary for his or her physical health . . .and praying for an order requiring the mother to submit to a caesarean section.

[T]he Court concludes and finds as a matter of law . . .this child is a viable human being and entitled to the protection of the Juvenile Court Code of Georgia. The Court concludes that this child is without the proper parental care and subsistence necessary for his or her physical life and health.

Temporary custody of the unborn child is hereby granted to the state of Georgia Department of Human Resources and the Butts County Department of Family and Children Services. The

Department shall have full authority to make all decisions, including giving consent to the surgical delivery appertaining to the birth of this child. The temporary custody of the Department shall terminate when the child has been successfully brought from its mother's body into the world or until the child dies, whichever shall happen.

Because of the unique nature of these cases, the powers of the Superior Court of Butts County are invoked and the defendant, Jessie Mae Jefferson, is hereby Ordered to submit to a sonogram (ultrasound) at the Griffin Spalding County Hospital or some other place which may be chosen by her where such procedure can be given. Should said sonogram indicate to the attending physician that the complete placenta previa is still blocking the child's passage into this world, Jessie Mae Jefferson is Ordered to submit to a caesarean section and related procedures considered necessary by the attending physician to sustain the life of this child.

The Court finds that the State has an interest in the life of this unborn living human being. The Court finds that the intrusion involved into the life of Jessie Mae Jefferson and her husband, John W. Jefferson, is outweighed by the duty of the State to protect a living, unborn human being from meeting his or her death before being given the opportunity to live . . . .

The parents filed their motion for stay at about 5.30 p.m. on January 23rd and after hearing oral argument . . . . this Court entered the following order on the evening of January 23:

[I]t is ordered that the Motion for Stay filed in this matter is hereby denied. The trial court's orders are effective immediately.

Hill P. J. stated that:

The power of a court to order a competent adult to submit to surgery is exceedingly limited. Indeed, until this unique case arose, I would have thought such power to be non-existent. Research shows that the courts generally have held that a competent adult had the right to refuse necessary life-saving surgery and medical treatment (i.e., has the right to die) where no state interest other than saving the life of the patient is involved. . . . On the other hand, one court has held that an expectant mother in the last weeks of pregnancy lacks the right to refuse necessary life-saving surgery and medical treatment

where the life of the unborn child is at stake. *Raleigh Fitkin-Paul Morgan Memorial Hospital v Anderson* (42 N.J. 421)....
In denying the stay of the trial court's order and thereby clearing the way for immediate re-examination by sonogram and probably for surgery, we weighed the right of the mother to practise her religion and to refuse surgery on herself, against her unborn child's right to live. We found in favour of her child's right to live.

Smith J, in a concurring judgement, held that:

[I]n the instant case, it appears that there is no less burdensome alternative for preserving the life of a fully developed fetus than requiring its mother to undergo surgery against her religious convictions. Such an intrusion by the state would be extraordinary, presenting some medical risk to both the mother and the fetus. However, the state's compelling interest in preserving the life of this fetus is beyond dispute.

Subsequent to the court's decision, but before any action was taken, Jessie Mae Jefferson gave birth naturally to her child.

2.   In San Diego, California, on 26 September 1986, Pamela Rae Stewart was arrested and charged under a statute of 1872 with causing her son's death by failing to obtain adequate medical care during pregnancy.[4] She had placenta previa, a condition which blocks part of the cervix leading to a risk of haemorrhage and oxygen deprivation of the child. She ignored medical advice to stop taking amphetamines, to refrain from sexual intercourse and delayed going to hospital for 'many hours'[5] after the onset of bleeding and contractions. The baby was born alive but with severe brain damage and died after six weeks. The California statute[6] penalises a 'parent of a minor child [who] wilfully omits, without lawful excuse, to furnish necessary ... medical attendance or other remedial care for his or her child'. The statute had been amended in 1925 to provide that 'a child conceived but not yet born ... [is] an existing person'.

The case against Stewart was dismissed. It was held that the statute did not cover the particular situation, in that no proof had been offered that medical attendance had not been sought or furnished.[7] The dismissal did not, however, come before the case had attracted national attention. Equally, it did not come before

Stewart had gone through the inevitable trauma associated with the loss of her child and the subsequent prosecution.[8]

3. On 10 November 1987, the Court of Appeals of the District of Colombia, in the case of Angela C.,[9] approved the lower court's order that a caesarean section be carried out on a terminally ill woman with hours or days to live, despite her apparent refusal of permission.[10] The child was in its 26th week of gestation. The mother was heavily sedated and *in extremis* suffering from a metastatic oxygenic carcinoma in her lung. The operation was performed. The child died two hours thereafter. The mother died two days later. The court in upholding the order held that 'the trial judge did not err in subordinating A.C.'s right against bodily intrusion to the interests of the unborn, [but potentially viable] child'. This was particularly so, the court held, because 'caesarean section would not *significantly* affect A.C.'s condition because she had, at best, two days left of sedated life'.[11] Obviously, 'significantly' assumes great significance here.

Commenting on this and other cases, Mahawold reports that out of 15 such applications to court, 14 were granted, although not all of them involved subsequent intervention because the mother was persuaded ultimately to consent, albeit under duress.[12]

4. In the case of Baby R,[13] the Provincial Court of British Columbia, in August 1988, approved the 'apprehension' of a 34-week-old fetus under the Family and Child Services Act which gives the Superintendent of Family and Child Services jurisdiction to 'apprehend' a child 'in need of protection'. The attending doctor took the view that 'a caesarean section was necessary because of the likely complications with a natural birth and the real danger of injury to the child, or death, with a normal birth. The mother declined to consent to a caesarean section.' The Superintendent thereupon decided to proceed with the purported apprehension. This was so as to give some sort of legality to the proposed performance of the caesarean section, contrary to the wishes of the mother who was already in labour. In the face of the order the woman subsequently agreed to the caesarean section, 'practically at the door of the operating room', but it would be hard to argue that she did so voluntarily. The Supreme Court of British Columbia subsequently overruled the decision, relying for their reasoning on the English case of *Re F (in utero)*.[14] '[T]he powers of the Superintendent to

apprehend are restricted', the Court decided, 'to living children that have been delivered. Were it otherwise, then the state would be able to confine a mother to await her delivery of the child being apprehended.'[15]

5. Dawn Johnsen writes that the San Diego case was

> only the most recent manifestation of a broader trend in which the state and other third parties increasingly are asserting what they perceive as the interests of the fetus in an attempt to use the law to dictate how women must behave during pregnancy .... A New Jersey statute seems to allow [she goes on] the state to seize custody of an 'unborn child' on the ground that the pregnant woman's behavior is endangering her fetus' welfare. A Los Angeles juvenile court did just that when it ordered that a woman who allegedly had an undiagnosed mental illness be detained for the last two months of her pregnancy. On appeal, a higher court found that the detention was improper: the statute on which the juvenile court had relied applied only to children. . . . By then, however, the woman had given birth and been released, and the court dismissed the case as moot.[16]

Nancy Rhoden equally expresses alarm at 'The potential for far-reaching state control of pregnant women ... suggested by the frightening array of prenatal interventions that some proponents of fetal protection advocate.'[17]

6, And lest you think this is a peculiarly North American phenomenon at the level of public action, recall first the warning of Nigel Lowe in 1987 that the use of wardship jurisdiction to limit the *mother's* behaviour could involve her being ordered, for example, 'to stop smoking or imbibing alcohol and indeed any activity which might be hazardous to the child' and could even involve the court in being faced with saving the fetus rather than the mother.[18] Then, recall the case of *D* v. *Berkshire CC*,[19] which concerned a baby girl born with drug withdrawal symptoms to a mother who was dependent on drugs. The House of Lords held that Berkshire Social Services Department were entitled to take the child into care *at birth*, because of the mother's prior neglect coupled with the threat of future neglect. As Fortin writes,

> The child's physical state at her birth which had necessitated her reception into intensive care for several weeks was the direct

result of her drug-addicted mother's persistent and excessive use of drugs during her pregnancy.

Such a short summary of the case, Fortin goes on

should not disguise its importance. Thus, whilst doctors will be unperturbed by the suggestion that a child's existence does not commence at birth and that its antenatal development should not be ignored, it is a well-established principle of law that a child does not obtain an independent legal status until it is born. Nevertheless, the House of Lords' willingness to consider the mother's antenatal behaviour was a clear acknowledgement that in certain circumstances, the law may quite properly concern itself with the appropriate treatment of unborn children.[20]

In *Re F (in utero)*,[21] another social services department attempted to *ward* a child *in utero* because of fears concerning the mother's capacity to manage her pregnancy safely. The local authority sought an order from the court under wardship jurisdiction *inter alia* directing that the court's tipstaff seek out the mother and request that she reside in a particular place and attend a particular hospital during pregnancy. An order was also sought giving the local authority care and control of the child when it was born. The mother was well-known to the local authority. She had a history of mental illness and drug use. Her first child had been subject to a care order, was living with foster parents and was due to be adopted. She had previously lived a nomadic existence and her disappearance when pregnant again prompted the local authority to take the unprecedented step of seeking to persuade the court to ward the unborn child. Hollings J refused to extend the wardship jurisdiction in this way. His decision was affirmed by the Court of Appeal. Balcombe and Staughton LJJ based their rejection of the application largely on the potential consequences of deciding otherwise, not least the limitations it would place on the mother and the difficulties of enforcement of any order. May LJ, however, was far more bullish: 'this is a case in which, on the facts, I would exercise the jurisdiction if I had it, [but] in the absence of authority I am driven to the conclusion that the court does not have the jurisdiction contended for'.[22]

A third English case we should notice is *Re P*.[23] Here again was a mother known to the local authority. She had had five children. Four were in care. The fifth had died soon after birth, after the local authority, under a Place of Safety Order, had removed it from the mother. The mother was pregnant again and was told that the baby once born would also be made subject to a Place of Safety Order. Anxious to prevent this and thereby keep the child, the mother started wardship proceedings while still pregnant, seeking thereby to outflank the local authority. Ewbank J dismissed the mother's application on the basis that *Re F* had established that 'as a matter of principle there is no jurisdiction at the present time in the High Court to make an unborn child a ward of court'.[24]

A paradigm for analysis

To complete the scene-setting, let me add to the circumstances which have already attracted the attention of the law, some indication of the breadth and range of factual circumstances which can pose the problems we are interested in. Only when we have seen these and understand them can we begin to understand the nature of the analysis which we must embark upon. Robertson and Schulman, in a very important paper in the Hastings Center Report in 1987[25] (a paper which I gratefully rely on), uses as a paradigm for analysis the case of a mother with maternal PKU. This involves the following: a mother, when a newborn, is born with PKU, which involves the inability to metabolise phenylalanine. If untreated, severe retardation will follow. If placed on a diet low in phenylalanine for at least five to seven years, retardation is prevented. When such a woman reaches adulthood and becomes pregnant she is at great risk of having a baby who will become severely retarded while still *in utero*. The risk arises because the phenylalanine which she continues to produce, but cannot metabolise, crosses the placenta. The fetus does not lack the enzyme necessary to metabolise its own phenylalanine but cannot deal with the mother's as well. Hence, the fetus is overwhelmed with phenylalanine and harmed *in utero* as a consequence. If the woman, before, or as early as possible after pregnancy, resumes the special diet low in phenylalanine which she had as a child, evidence suggests that the problem can be avoided. But this means that she must adhere strictly for nine months to what is an unpleasant diet. Most women will, of course, gladly do so, but what of the woman who is feckless or simply refuses? As Robertson reminds us, 'the mother's normal diet acts like a toxin on the fetus, damaging it just as ingesting alcohol, cocaine, heroin or other drugs might'.[26] What, to remind you of our opening question, are the mother's rights and responsibilities in such a case?

There are, of course, other factual circumstances which are more familiar to us. Avoidable prenatal injuries or death may arise from the abuse of alcohol, heroin or other substances, from exposure to environmental hazards, particularly in the workplace, from contraction of herpes, syphilis or HIV infection, and, of course, from refusal to undergo prenatal medical or surgical treatment, e.g. blood transfusion in the case of rhesus negativity or a caesarean section.

Indeed, surveying such a scene and recognising the potential extent of the limits which could be placed on a mother's freedom of action, John Robertson was moved to write eight years ago that pregnant women

> may also be prohibited from using alcohol or other substances harmful to the fetus during pregnancy, or be kept from the workplace because of toxic effects on the fetus. They could be ordered to take drugs, such as insulin for diabetes, medications for fetal deficiencies, or intra-uterine blood transfusion for Rh factor. Pregnant anorexic teen-agers could be force fed. Prenatal screening and diagnostic procedures, from amniocentesis to sonography or even fetoscopy could be made mandatory. And *in utero* surgery for the fetus to shunt cerebroventricular fluids from the brain to relieve hydrocephalus, or to relieve the urethral obstruction of bilateral hydronephrosis could also be ordered. Indeed, even extra-uterine fetal surgery, if it becomes an established procedure, could be ordered, if the risks to the mother were small and it were a last resort to save the life or prevent severe disability in a viable fetus.[27]

The significance of the problem

These examples set the scene of our discussion. They pose, as you realise, very difficult problems which will only multiply as time goes on. In seeking to resolve them, we must notice three things. First, the problems posed are sometimes characterised as conflicts between the mother and her fetus, whereby they are seen as adversaries. It is important to realise this is not necessarily so. As we have seen, the mother may insist on a course of action which she realises is against her own interests as well as the interests of the fetus but which she feels she is obliged to follow. Thus, an analytical model which assumes that mother and fetus are *ex hypothesi* adversaries may be unhelpful. The second point to notice is that clearly the issue is not trivial. Indeed, it is likely to grow in importance and significance. Developments in medical technology and knowledge make this inevitable as do the changes in society's concern for the fetus and consequently the political climate concerning, for example, abortion. Thirdly, it is also clear that the issue is very charged. George Annas, writing a paper in the Hastings Center Report, critical of the San Diego case, used the title 'Pregnant Women as Fetal Containers'[28] and quoted Margaret Atwood's, *The Handmaid's Tale*, in which one handmaid describes her station as 'we are two-legged wombs, that's all; sacred vessels, ambulatory chalices'.[29] Dawn Johnsen, also in the Hastings Center Report, wrote of a 'New Threat to Pregnant Women's Autonomy'.[30] And many feminists (not, it should be remembered, a homogenous group) condemn even raising the issue as being discriminatory, not least because it involves considering women's rights in terms of their child-bearing capacities. Obviously, the arguments about the 'woman as chattel', or 'the woman enslaved by society once pregnant' are just as much to the fore here as in the context of abortion.

Points for analysis

So, with these points in mind, how should we proceed? An examination of the facts suggest that we can identify at least five variables or points for analysis, as being critical if we are going to conduct a careful enquiry. They are:

(a) The nature of the risk, or threat, to the fetus. Clearly, there is a wide variation. It may be death or it may be disability, and if the latter, it may be serious or less so.

(b) The causal link between the conduct of the mother and the risk to the fetus. The facts suggest that the link may be more or less tenuous, (alerting us to arguments about slippery slopes).

(c) The time-frame involved. This can be exensive or short. In the case of maternal PKU, the restriction on the mother's choice lasts for nine months. By contrast, in the case of a caesarean section, it will be a matter of hours.

(d) The stage of development of the fetus. The facts indicate that a problem may arise at various stages of fetal development. The fetus may have a gestational age of only a few weeks, it may be viable, or it may be virtually at full term.

(e) The degree of limitation on the woman's choice, (I avoid here the language of 'freedom' as it may affect the subsequent analysis). It is clear from the facts that the degree of limitation may fall to be assessed both in terms of length of time (as suggested above), and of what the mother is called upon to do, e.g. undergo surgery or deny her religious convictions.

Analysis

Let us now begin our analysis. Analyse we must, as a first step to arriving at policy options. This, you will recall, is my concern: the making of good public policy in the face of real medical-moral dilemmas. I intend to ask what the woman is morally entitled, and obliged, to do and then to ask whether, in the light of this, some public policy is called for and how this policy should be expressed, one form being *law*.

Moral theory

Unhelpful arguments

Let me first consider the issue in terms of moral theory. The question for analysis is whether there is any justification in arguing that a woman is *morally* obliged to submit to a certain regime or intervention, or has a duty to do so. Let me get out of the way two arguments which are unhelpful. The first has it that if we admit, as many do (and the law allows) that abortion, at least in certain circumstances, is permissible, it is contradictory to talk of obliging a woman to submit to a caesarean section or other such medical intervention. Put crudely, if the mother can kill the fetus by abortion, then she must be entitled to do anything to the fetus which amounts to less than killing it. This is a bad argument. It confuses what is at stake. We are not concerned here with the fetus's interest in being born, or society's interest in its being born. We are, instead, concerned with the issue of the fetus's interest in its being born free of avoidable harm when the mother has decided not to abort but to carry the fetus and, all things being equal, to bring it to term.[31]

Now let us turn to the second unhelpful argument. Can we not solve all our questions, it is asked, by saying that the doctor has two patients and that he is justified in protecting his second patient, the fetus (and that we are justified in supporting him). This is unhelpful because it begs the two questions which are central to our debate. The first is, what is the status of the fetus? Is it an entity which is owed duties, i.e. *is* it, or can it be, a patient? The second is, even if it is a patient, why should its interests prevail? How are the duties owed to it to be reconciled with the duties owed to the mother? These are precisely the questions we have to answer.

Fetal rights

With those points out of the way, let us proceed. I take as a starting point the uncontentious proposition that a woman (including a pregnant woman) has a right to autonomy, of which the right to privacy and to be free from unwanted bodily interference is one important aspect. Such a right to autonomy is, of course, only a *prima facie* right. Its enjoyment may, as a matter of principle, have to give way, in appropriate circumstances, to the rights of others. Obviously, the seriousness with which we regard respect for autonomy leads us to be vigilant in demanding justification for any limitations or restrictions. But, none the less, examples are part of our daily life. A woman who poses a threat to the safety of others is an obvious example.

Is the fetus here a relevant other with rights? Does the fetus have rights which may, in appropriate circumstances, limit the mother's right to autonomy? My position is that a fetus *is* a relevant other and that it does have rights. We may call them weak rights, if you will, since they may pertain to an entity not yet (and perhaps never) independent of its mother and whose fate is inextricably connected to hers. We may also recognise that they are rights which grow stronger as the fetus develops, since at some point, although still *in utero*, the fetus becomes capable of independent existence. Finally, we may recognise that to state that the fetus has rights is not to deny that until born they may always be defeasible, if 'trumped' by the mother's rights for good reason. Notwithstanding these caveats, I return to my central proposition, that a fetus has rights.

What follows from this? It is my position that, if the fetus does have rights as a matter of moral argument, these rights must include the right of the fetus to be free from avoidable harm, to be free from that which may destroy or damage its potential for being born whole.

Maternal duties

To take the argument a step further, talk of fetus's rights allows us to assert in turn that the mother owes the fetus certain duties. The primary duty is, perhaps, the duty not to interfere with the fetus's rights, including the right to be born free from avoidable harm, save for good reason. In practical terms, this translates into a duty not to expose the fetus to avoidable harm intentionally, recklessly, or negligently, whether by doing something, e.g. dangerous conduct, or by refraining from doing something, e.g. refusing necessary medical care. Robertson helpfully captures the duty as follows: a duty not to engage in 'avoidable conduct that falls below reasonable community standards, after notice and counselling [whereby the] offspring [is] seriously and wilfully harmed'.[32] These latter two conditions are important as indicating that the mother's duty attaches when she is aware of the risk she may pose. I would suggest, however, that there are circumstances in which she may be expected to be aware of the risk, e.g. in the case of abuse of drugs. It is, of course, a question for debate how serious the harm must be, e.g. death, serious disability or some relatively trivial inconvenience, before the mother is *prima facie* under a duty to limit her conduct. Once she is under such a duty, however, the duty must be observed unless there are good reasons for not doing so.

A *calculus*

If my conclusion is that limits *do* exist morally to the freedom of action of the mother, the next stage in our analysis must be to ask how this abstract proposition may translate into guidance in dealing with the type of factual circumstances already discussed. Under what circumstances in concrete cases will a mother's freedom of action be limited? This is not, of course, a question to be answered by some sort of checklist, whereby in each case a specific decision, one way or the other, can be reached. The enquiry is too subtle. Instead, the only approach, as in any other enquiry in applied ethics, is to identify in abstract terms what appear to be the factors which are morally relevant in the light of the competing moral claims which have been set out. The result is not a simple (or simple-minded) either/or system. Instead, it is some sort of calculus. Resort to this calculus will provide guidance for decisions or action, though it will not, of course, resolve any specific case. The elements of the calculus, which you will notice echoes the variables I mentioned earlier, are:

(a) The nature of the harm which the fetus may be exposed to. The more serious the harm, the more compelling may be the mother's duty and the greater the need on the part of the mother to show compelling reasons for not complying with it.

(b) The capacity of the mother to comply with the conduct or regime deemed appropriate to protect the fetus. Account must be taken, for example, of such matters as the availability of medical and other care, access the mother has to such care, the level of her education and knowledge, the relative poverty in which she finds herself, and her capacity to exercise freewill rather than being, for example, dependent on drugs.

(c) A demonstrable relationship between the conduct of the mother (whether it be action or inaction) and the threatened harm to the fetus. This is a matter of medical evidence and advice. The more tenuous the link (e.g. the link alleged between smoking or jogging and early fetal harm), or the earlier in pregnancy the mother engages in a certain conduct, the less the duty can be said to limit the mother.

(d) The relative development of the fetus. The more developed the fetus the greater may be its moral claim and the more limited may be the mother's freedom of action.

(e) The degree of limitation on the mother's choice. The limitation may range from an obligation to undergo a specific diet for nine months, to abstain from smoking, to abstain from some other substance or conduct, to be detained in a specific place under a specific regime, to undergo a medical procedure or to undergo surgical intervention. The greater the limitation, the greater must be the claim of the fetus.

(f) The risk to the mother's health, e.g. from a proposed surgical intervention. The more serious the risk associated with the proposed intervention or other stipulated regime, the less strong may be the claim of the fetus.

(g) The reasons for the mother's choice or conduct. It may range from mere convenience to religious conviction, concern for her own health or concern for the fetus's or future child's health. That is to say, it may range from the trivial to the serious. The more trivial it is, the less justified the mother may be in seeking to rely on it.

(h) The recognised uncertainty of prenatal diagnosis. The greater the grounds for uncertainty, the less it may serve as a ground for limiting the mother's freedom of action.[33]

The significant features of this calculus are that, first, it allows the fetus to enter the equation and have its interests considered and, secondly, it then offers the means of assessing the competing claims of the mother and the fetus. It entails the conclusion that, when all is taken into account, if the case for the fetus is strong and the reasons for the mother's conduct are weak or less strong, she has a duty as a matter of moral theory to submit to the stipulated regime or treatment. This is so, whether it be a specific diet or drug prescription, abstinence from a particular substance or conduct, or some intervention such as a blood transfusion or even surgery.

Enter the law

Consequences of requiring maternal compliance

Does this mean, however that *others* can then *require* the mother to comply with her duty to the fetus, if resort to this calculus indicates that morally she should? To decide that others may require or compel her to do so, has, of course, contingent consequences which go beyond the limitation of the particular woman's choice. These consequences are by no means trivial. The image of 'the woman enslaved' reappears. Grave difficulties exist concerning the enforcement of any limitation. Guilt may be engendered in mothers generally, anxious about the merest deviation from the prescribed norm of conduct. Resentment towards childbearing could equally be engendered. Allegations of unfair discrimination against women could be made.[34] Finally, mothers could become reluctant to seek antenatal care.

Making public policy

These consequences, if thought to be sufficiently serious or real, may have considerable implications for public policy. They may persuade the policy-maker or the analyst not to go beyond the level of moral argument, beyond the assertion that mothers owe a moral duty which they ought to comply with. Alternatively, the policy-maker or analyst may say that these contingent consequences are serious but less serious than the risk to the fetus, and consequent unborn child, if no further step by way of formulation of public policy is taken. They may conclude that some further step is called for.

If we are to consider others *requiring* maternal compliance, we are inevitably moving from a moral analysis to a consideration of the law, since interference with the liberties of another is ordinarily impermissible, unless specifically provided for by law. Otherwise it is unlawful. Of course, the first and obvious method whereby others can seek to require maternal compliance is through counselling, education and persuasion. These are obviously the most desirable routes to take and can represent a significant public policy statement in themselves. Furthermore, they do not call for reliance on the law. But, if we assume that persuasion and education have failed, what then? If we are to consider the law, two questions arise. What does the existing law provide? Secondly, should the law be changed if it fails to strike the appropriate balance between the moral claims of mother and fetus?

In considering these questions, there are obviously two circumstances which the law could address and regulate: while the mother is still pregnant and the fetus is *in utero* and, secondly, when the baby is born. The former more clearly involves the sort of limitation of a mother's freedom of action which we have been discussing. The latter form of regulation, however, by, for example, applying some sort of sanction after birth (as in the San Diego case) could, of course, ultimately have the same sort of limiting effect. If women know, or fear, that once the child is born they will suffer some sanction, e.g. the loss of custody of the child, this will inevitably affect the choices they will make during pregnancy.

So, let us examine what English law has to say about these two potential responses, what Robertson with his eye for the telling phrase calls 'pre-birth seizure' (taking control of the woman) and 'post-birth sanction' (punishing a particular woman and deterring others).[35]

(a)   Pre-birth seizure

The pre-birth limitation of a woman's freedom of action, whether by requiring her to do something or refrain from doing something, has its supporters. Keyserlingk argues that,

> Unless 'armed' with juridical personality as the basis of his right to care and protection, the unborn child would be (as is now the case) unable to compete on a more or less equal basis with other parties with whom his needs and rights may be in conflict. They would be legal persons and he would remain more or less at the mercy of their ethics, whims or compassions.... Since the unborn child has health needs and vulnerabilities analogous to those of healthy children, and since between the child when unborn and after birth there is continuity in all essential respects, then it would seem logical and just to assign to parents duties to their unborn children analogous (when applicable) to those they have to their children, and to recognise unborn children analogous rights (when applicable) to those already granted to children.[36]

Notwithstanding this view, pre-birth seizure does not appear to be permitted in English law, either by statute or case law.

1. Statute law.   At present there is no statute in English law which governs the particular situation under consideration. There are, of course, statutes which permit the seizure of a citizen, for example, for the purposes of arrest,[37] or detention, or even treatment, in the case of mental disorder, provided certain conditions are satisfied,[38] or seizure to recover evidence of a crime.[39] None of these covers the case in question. Nor is it permissable to argue from these statutes by analogy, if only because there is a presumption in law that the liberty of a citizen may not ordinarily be infringed save when specifically provided for by statute.[40]

2. Common law.   Recent cases have decided that a fetus has no legal status in English law. Thus, any attempt to seek to persuade a court to protect or enforce a fetus's rights as against those of its mother would not succeed. In the landmark decision of *Paton* v. *Tustees of BPAS*,[41] Sir George Baker P stated that 'The fetus cannot, in English law, in my view have a right of its own until it is born and has a separate existence from its mother.'[42] The subsequent cases of *C* v. *S*,[43] *D* v. *Berkshire CC*[44] and *Re F* (*in utero*)[45] have, as we have seen, reiterated this conclusion. Put another way, echoing the language of state's interests found in the USA, the state in English law has no interest in protecting or preserving the rights

of the fetus. Thus, the use of the law relating to child neglect, canvassed in the USA, fails in English law since the fetus is not a legal person, i.e. not a child within the relevant law. Nor will wardship jurisdiction extend to a fetus, as we have seen. Balcombe LJ put it in the following terms in the case of *Re F*,

> since an unborn child has, *ex hypothesi* no existence indepen-
> dent of its mother, the only purpose of extending the jurisdic-
> tion to include the fetus is to enable the mother's actions to be
> controlled. Indeed, that is the purpose of the present applica-
> tion. . . . [I]t would be intolerable to place a judge in the position
> of having to make such a decision [to consent to a caesarean
> section] without any guidance as to the principles on which his
> decision should be based. If the law is to be extended in this
> manner, so as to impose control over the mother of an unborn
> child, where such control may be necessary for the benefit of
> that child, then under our system of parliamentary democracy it
> is for Parliament to decide whether such controls can be im-
> posed and, if so, subject to what limitations or conditions.[46]

Is the criminal law relevant here? It does not appear to be a crime in English law to refrain from doing something that may protect a fetus from avoidable harm, or to do something which exposes a fetus to avoidable harm, on the basis that since abortion is allowed, the greater includes the lesser. What of the Infant Life (Preserva-tion) Act 1929? Is it not of some relevance, at least after the fetus is 'capable of being born alive?'[47] Section 1(1) of the Act provides that 'any person who, with the intent to destroy the life of a child capable of being born alive, by any wilful act causes a child to die before it has an existence independent of its mother, shall be guilty. . .'. The obvious difficulties in the way of any successful prosecution of a mother include the need to prove intent, the need for a wilful *act* rather than an omission and the need to show that the act complained of *caused* death. These seem insuperable prob-lems in the sort of factual circumstances which have arisen in decided cases or have been raised by commentators. It is hard to argue that the mother who smokes, drinks alcohol, takes drugs or continues to engage in sexual intercourse 'intends to destroy the life of [her] child'. Is there a wilful act (leave aside intent to destroy) when a mother refuses a blood transfusion or caesarean section? In any event, whatever the answers to the specific points may be, the Act is only concerned with the viable fetus. Prosecution under the Act does not help the fetus, and it certainly does not allow 'pre-birth seizure'.

The conclusion must be that, as regards the current state of English case law, any doctor who engages in any medical intervention on the mother without her consent, albeit for the benefit of the unborn baby she is carrying, or anyone who, for the same reason, restrains her or restricts her freedom of action would be guilty of a crime and also liable in damages. There would, in other words, be no justification available in law.

No contemporary review of English law in this context is complete, however, without reference to the European Convention on Human Rights. Article 2(1) begins, 'Everyone's right to life shall be protected'. Obviously, the applicability of this Article turns on whether a fetus is to be recognised as having a 'right to life' within the terms of Article 2. The European Court of Human Rights has yet to take a view on this point. The European Commission of Human Rights in *Paton* v. *United Kingdom*[48] chose to leave the question undecided. Were the court to decide that the fetus does have such a right to life, albeit not an absolute right,[49] it could go on to decide that, in a particular case, the fetus's right could take priority over the mother's wishes, otherwise protected by her 'right to privacy' under Article 8, save, in the case where the fetus posed a real threat to the mother's life.

Before leaving this discussion of pre-birth seizure, it may be instructive, finally, to notice a striking, and some would say clinching, argument which sums up the legal analysis here and is offered by a number of commentators in the USA. It is as follows. Insofar as no one is obliged in law to, for example, donate a kidney or bone marrow to someone else (see *McFall* v. *Shimp*[50]) (although someone may be said to have a moral obligation to do so), it must follow that a mother is not obliged to save the life of a fetus if she chooses not to. There can be no justification, the argument goes, in placing greater obligations on her as regards her unborn child than are placed on others in respect of saving or helping the life of a third party. Rhoden writes of a 'primal revulsion. . . . at a person's or government's sacrificing one person to benefit others'.[51] She cites approvingly the view of the distinguished commentator Professor Tribe, 'that one person's two good eyes, distributed to two blind neighbours, might yield a net increase in happiness on the theory that one blind person will experience less misery than two, cannot justify a governmental decision to compel the exchange'.[52] 'Were there a serious risk of the woman's suffering permanent harm from the [caesarean] surgery', Rhoden concludes, 'requiring it would seem too much like [this example], where our intuitions strongly tell us that such decisions are ethically impermissible.'[53] George Annas makes the point succinctly: 'No mother has ever been legally required to undergo surgery or general anaesthetic (e.g. bone marrow aspiration) to save the life of her dying child. It would be ironic and unfair if she could be forced to submit to more invasive surgical procedures for the sake of her fetus than for her child.'[54]

It could be said that the vulnerability of the fetus and the lack of any alternative form of possible assistance for the fetus may make the *moral* force of the argument less strong. But these factors should have no weight in any *legal* analysis since the fact that a fetus is not a person in law means its claim is not recognised. Furthermore, if the argument is not to prevail it could be said that the law was adopting a position which was adversely discriminatory towards women.[55]

That said, it is not, of course, a clinching argument in all circumstances. It may argue powerfully against surgical interventions, but it is not clear that it is so persuasive an argument as regards less intrusive limitations on the mother. Its relevance here is to suggest that not only does English law at present not permit pre-birth seizure, but also, should the issue be raised, good arguments exist to reject it.

(b)   Post-birth sanction

Does existing English law allow such a sanction to punish the mother and thereby deter her and others?

1. Statute law.   I take the circumstances contemplated by post-birth sanction to be that a mother has given birth to her child. The child may, however, have been born disabled or have died as a consequence of the mother's conduct while pregnant. Does the criminal law make any provision for post-birth sanction? Is the mother guilty of any crime in such a situation? Clearly, the Infant Life (Preservation) Act 1929 has no application. Nor, it appears, does any other statutory provision of the criminal law.

What of the Children and Young Persons Act 1969, which allows a local authority by s. 1(2) to take a child into care if the relevant conditions are satisfied? Recall that the question asked is whether this Act may be used by a local authority as a post-birth sanction against behaviour of the mother while pregnant. Superficially, *D* v. *Berkshire CC*[56] would appear to suggest that the Act was used to sanction the drug-addicted mother, and thereby deter others, by taking her child into care at birth. But this is not, in fact, what the House of Lords decided. As Lord Goff was at pains to point out, the child was not being taken into care because of what had happened in the past. Care proceedings could not be justified on those grounds alone. The court had to be satisfied that 'there is an existing likelihood that the state of affairs revealed by those past events *will continue into the future*'.[57] The Children and Young Persons Act 1969 is not, therefore, available as a sanction against maternal conduct during pregnancy. Equally, tort law offers no remedy. The Congenital Disabilities (Civil Liability) Act 1976 was passed to provide a remedy to children harmed through negligently caused prenatal injury. But, the Act imposes liability on the *mother* only in the context of driving a motor vehicle.[58] Only in such a case can it be guaranteed that the mother is insured. In all other cases, the mother is immune from liability. Post-birth sanction again, therefore, does not exist.

2. Common law. There is no precedent at common law for applying a post-birth sanction to a woman, whether by civil action or otherwise. Nor, given the state of the law and the likely response of judges, is there likely to be one.

The conclusion must be, therefore, that the existing state of English law does not allow for either of the two options Robertson identified as ways of giving effect to any moral claims of the fetus.

Change the law?

If the law is to be invoked on behalf of a fetus, if a mother is to be required to do, or refrain from doing, something, the law must be changed. A court, theoretically, could decide to act. But, given the weight of legal argument that the courts have no power to do so, Parliament would have to act. Is this likely?

Undoubtedly, given developments in medical knowledge and technology and the climate of the times, concern over the sort of factual situations we have been discussing will only grow. Calls for some sort of action will become more common. The first response of government should, and no doubt will, be to continue its long-standing commitment to public education and to raising the awareness of women, both as to their responsibilities and to the risks posed by certain conduct. Equally, government could be persuaded, and may be willing, to invest appropriate resources in antenatal care and counselling, and generally to encourage respect for, and the self-esteem of, mothers.

But, these policies, desirable and necessary as they are, may not be enough. We would then have to return to the law.

At one level, there is no doubt that the law *could* be changed to achieve either pre-birth seizure or post-birth sanction or both. At this level it is really a question of drafting. Parliament could amend the Infant Life (Preservation) Act so as to capture and criminalise such conduct of the mother as it thought appropriate. Likewise, the Children and Young Persons Act could be amended to allow a local authority to obtain a care order while the fetus is still *in utero* or at birth, so as to serve as a post-birth sanction. The wardship jurisdiction could be extended to protect the fetus simply by amending s. 41 of the Supreme Court Act 1981, so that the word 'minor' used in that section, was made explicitly to refer to the unborn child.[59] And so on.

But, this is not really the question. While Parliament could make these specific legislative changes, should it do so? We have seen that in terms of moral analysis there is a case, in certain circumstances, for limiting a mother's freedom of action. We have also seen, however, the contingent social consequences which may flow from doing this by means of law. These would perhaps take on even greater significance if the approach adopted was to make interstitial amendments to existing legislation. The weakness of this approach is that it obscures or does not make explicit the process of weighing competing claims which is at the heart of the endeavour. By so doing, it would lend weight to the arguments of those who say that the sole effect of changes in the law is to oppress or discriminate against women.

One solution may be as follows. The calculus advanced earlier by way of moral analysis could just as readily serve as the basis for legal analysis. A judge could hear the arguments, consider the evidence and, having weighed the relative claims of mother and fetus, decide what was to be done in any particular case. A law could be drafted, in other words, to give a judge the power to order pre-birth seizure or post-birth sanction (whether it involves surgery, wardship of the unborn or a care order at birth) in an appropriate case, i.e. one in which the calculus weighs sufficiently heavily in favour of the fetus's claims.

It is, of course, a matter for legitimate difference whether the undesirable consequences which could flow from such a piece of legislation, not least the perceived oppression of women left to the whim of a mainly male judiciary, are outweighed by the good which may be produced. It must not be overlooked, however, that such legislation, if it were passed, could have a further effect. Unless it was tightly drawn it may be seized on as a legislative precedent for the proposition that a fetus is a legal person. The implications of such a conclusion for the laws of abortion, and for women's rights over their own body, could be extremely far-reaching. Indeed, they may be so problematic that they tip the scales against any change in the existing law. It may well be possible for a judge to do the balancing called for by our moral analysis, provided we could draft a statute sufficiently carefully. It may not, however, be desirable. It may well be that we should continue to leave the fate of the unborn child to its mother and resist the call for legal regulation of her conduct. To do otherwise may cause us to pay just too high a price.

Notes and references

1. See for example, A. Grubb and D. Pearl, 'Protecting the Life of the Unborn Child, *Law Quarterly Review*, vol. 103 (1987) p. 340; B. Dimond, 'Consent, Compulsion and the Rights of the Mother and Unborn Child, *Midwives Chronicle and Nursing Notes*, vol. 99 (1987) p. 1179; J. Fortin, 'Legal Protection for the Unborn Child', *Modern Law Review*, vol. 5, (1988) p. 54, and 'Can you Ward a Foetus', *Modern Law Review*, vol. 51 (1988) p. 768; R. Gillon, 'Pregnancy, Obstetrics and the Moral Status of the Fetus', *Journal of Medical Ethics* vol. 14 (1988) p. 1.

2. See, for example, American College of Obstetrics and Gynaecologists, 'Patient Choice: Maternal–Fetal Conflict', *ACOG Committee Opinion* (1987); G. Annas, 'Pregnant Women as Fetal Containers', *Hastings Center Report*, vol. 16 (1986) p. 13, 'The Impact of Medical Technology on the Pregnant Woman's Right to Privacy', *American Journal of Legal Medicine*, vol. 13 (1987), and 'Protecting the Liberty of Pregnant Patients', *New England Journal of Medicine* vol. 316 (1987) p. 1214; R. Blank, 'Emerging Notions of Women's Rights and Responsibilities During Gestation', *Journal of Legal Medicine* vol. 7 (1986) p. 441; J. C. Fletcher, 'Emerging Ethical Issues in Fetal Therapy', *Progress in Clinical Biological Research* vol. 128 (1983) p. 293; J. Gallaher,

'Prenatal Invasion and Interventions: What's Wrong with Fetal Rights'. *Harvard Women's Law Journal*, vol. 10 (1987) p. 9; D. Johnsen, 'The Creation of Fetal Rights: Conflicts with Women's Constitutional Rights to Liberty, Privacy and Equal Protection', *Yale Law Journal*, vol. 7 (1986) p. 251, and 'A New Threat to Pregnant Women's Autonomy', *Hastings Center Report*, vol. 17 (1987) p. 33; M. Mahawold, 'Beyond Abortion: Refusal of Cesarean Section', *Bioethics*, vol. 3 (1989) p. 106; D. Mathieeu, 'Respecting Liberty and Preventing Harm: Limits of State Intervention on Prenatal Choice', *Harvard Journal of Law and Public Policy*, vol. 8 (1985) p. 19; L. Nelson and N. Milliken, 'Compelled Medical Treatment of Pregnant Women: Life, Liberty and Law in Conflict', *Journal of the American Medical Association*, vol. 259 (1988) p. 7; N. Rhoden 'The Judge in the Delivery Room: The Emergence of Court Ordered Cesareans', *California Law Review*, vol. 74 (1986) p. 1951; J. Robertson and J. D. Schulman, 'Pregnancy and Prenatal Harm to Offspring: The Case of Mothers with PKU', *Hastings Center Report*, vol. 17 (1987) p. 23; B. K. Rothman, *Recreating Motherhood* (New York: W. W Norton, 1989); G. Schedler, 'Women's Reproductive Rights: Is There a Conflict with a Child's Right to be Born Free from Defects?', *Journal of Legal Medicine*, vol. 7 (1986) p. 357; B. Steinbock, D. Marquis and S. Kayata. 'Case Studies – Preterm Labor and Prenatal Harm'. *Hastings Center Report*, vol. 19 (1989) p. 32.

3. 247 Ga. 86, 274 S.E. 2d 457.
4. See, for a detailed discussion, Annas, 'Pregnant Women', p. 13.
5. Ibid., citing the police report.
6. *California Penal Code*, s. 270 (West Publishing, St. Paul, Minn., 1986).
7. There is some disagreement about the grounds for the dismissal. Compare Robertson's and Johnsen's papers in the *Hastings Center Report*.
8. Johnsen comments in 'A New Threat': 'By the time Ms. Stewart's criminal prosecution was dismissed five months after her arrest . . . she had spent six days in jail. . . . During her prosecution the most intimate details of her life were repeatedly examined by the news media across the country.'
9. *Re A.C.,* D.C. Ct. App. 533, A 2d.611 (1987).
10. 'Before she was sedated, A. C. indicated that she would choose to relinquish her life so that the fetus could survive should such a choice present itself at the fetus' gestational age of twenty-eight weeks. Her physicians never discussed with her what her choice would be if such a choice had to be made before the fetus reached the twenty-eight week point. . . . Shortly after the trial judge made his decision [that the caesarean be performed], A. C. was informed of it. She stated, during a period of lucidity, that she would agree to the surgery although she might not survive it. When another physician went to A. C. to verify her decision, she apparently changed her mind, mouthing the words, "I don't want it done".' Ibid., *per* Nebeker AJ.
11. Ibid., *per* Nebeker AJ. *Re A.C.* was subsequently reheard *en banc* and the Court of Appeals issued a second judgement on April 26, 1990,

No. 87–609. . . . The Court vacated its prior order on the grounds that there had not been a proper finding of fact whether A.C. was competent, or, if she was not, how 'substituted judgement' was to be applied. The Court did, however, decide that the decision of a competent patient or substituted judgement should prevail, even if surgery was refused, in 'virtually all cases' unless there are 'truly extraordinary or compelling reasons to override them,' by taking account, for example, of the State's interest in protecting life. At the same time the Court did not dissent from, or overrule, a previous decision (1986) of the Superior Court in *Re Madyun* (unreported: published as Appendix to *Re A.C.*). In *Madyun*, the Court authorised surgery on a woman who objected for religious reasons. 'All that stood between the Madyun fetus and its independent existence was, put simply, a doctor's scalpel [sic]. In these circumstances, the life of the infant inside its mother's womb was entitled to be protected.'

12. Mahawold, 'Beyond Abortion', p. 113. She notes that, '[I]n the majority (88%) of reported requests for court orders, the order has been obtained in less than six hours, 19% have been granted in less than one hour, and at least one order has been granted by telephone'.

13. *Re Baby R* (unreported), No. A872582, Vancouver Register (Supreme Court of British Columbia).

14. [1988] 2 All ER 193, and see following discussion.

15. *Re Baby R* (unreported), No. A872582, Vancouver Register, *per* Macdonell J.

16. Johnsen, 'A New Threat', p. 34.

17. Rhoden 'The Judge', p. 2027.

18. N. V. Lowe pp. 29, 30, cited in Fortin, 'Can You Ward a Fetus', *Law Quarterly Review*, vol. 96, p. 772.

19. [1987] 1 All ER 20.

20. Fortin 'Legal Protection', p. 54.

21. [1988] 2 All ER 193.

22. Ibid., 196.

23. Unreported: a decision of Ewbank J., 28 March 1988. See, further, Fortin, 'Can You Ward a Fetus', p. 773–4.

24. Ibid.

25. Robertson and Schulman, 'Pregnancy and Prenatal Harm'.

26. Ibid., p. 24.

27. J. Robertson, 'The Right to Procreate and *in utero* Fetal Therapy', *Journal of Legal Medicine*, vol. 3 (1982) pp. 333, 358. It is important, however, to notice, by way of counterpoise to Robertson's warnings, the recent dramatic increase in the US of infant mortality due to maternal drug use. In the first half of 1989 there was a 50 per cent increase in infant mortality because of a surge in babies born to cocaine-addicted women. The rate was 32.3 deaths per 1000 live births, compared with 23.2 per 1000 in 1988 in Washington DC and 9.9 per 1000 in the USA overall. *Minneapolis Star Tribune*, 1 October 1989.

28. Annas, 'Pregnant Women'.

29. Ibid.

30. Johnsen, 'A New Threat'.
31. See Steinbock *et al.*, 'Case Studies', p. 32.
32. Robertson and Schulman, 'Pregnancy and Prenatal Harm', p. 28.
33. It will be recalled that in the Jefferson case which I began with, Jessie Mae Jefferson gave birth vaginally to a healthy baby while the case was being appealed. See further, Mahawold, 'Beyond Abortion', p. 119.
34. See, on these points and generally, Mahawold, 'Beyond Abortion'.
35. Robertson and Schulman, 'Pregnancy and Prenatal Harm', p. 29.
36. E. W. Keyserlingk, 'The Unborn Child's Right to Prenatal Care – A Comparative Law Perspective.' *McGill Legal Studies* vol. 5 (1984) pp. 79, 103.
37. The Police and Criminal Evidence Act 1984.
38. See Mental Health Act 1983, Part II.
39. The Police and Criminal Evidence Act 1984.
40. For a detailed analysis, from the point of view of U.S. law, of statutes authorising 'compulsory bodily invasions', see Rhoden, 'The Judge', pp. 1982–8. She concludes that such laws are designed to promote various state interests of a wholly different order from that under consideration. She refers to compulsory vaccination, intrusions to obtain evidence from criminal suspects and non-consensual treatment of institutionalised persons, all of which have been held to be constitutional. 'A brief examination of these cases', she goes on, 'will show that in no other area do courts countenance invasions as substantial as caesarean sections', ibid. The same conclusion may be drawn as regards statutes in English law.
41. [1979] QB 276.
42. Ibid., 279.
43. [1987] 1 All ER 1230.
44. [1987] 1 All ER 20.
45. [1988] 2 All ER 193.
46. Ibid., 200.
47. Section 1(1).
48. (1980) 3EHRR 408.
49. The European Commission of Human Rights in *Paton* v. *UK* (1980) 3EHRR 408 decided that, whatever the position as regards a claim to a qualified right to life, a fetus could not be said to enjoy an absolute right to life under Article 2.
50. 10 Pa. D & C 3d 90 (1978).
51. Rhoden, 'The Judge', p. 2002.
52. L. Tribe, *American Constitutional Law* (Mineola NY: Foundation Press, 1978) p. 918.
53. Rhoden, 'The Judge', p. 2002.
54. G. Annas, *Judging Medicine* (Clifton NJ: Humana Press, 1988) p. 122.
55. See Mahawold, 'Beyond Abortion', p. 118.
56. [1987] 1 All ER 20.
57. Ibid., 45.
58. Section 2.
59. Fortin, 'Can You Ward a Fetus', pp. 769–70.

Index